THE HAUNTED BOOKSHOP

A comedy thriller in two acts

Lynn Brittney

Adapted from the book of the same name
by Christopher Morley

Published by Playstage
United Kingdom.

An imprint of Write Publications Ltd

www.playsforadults.com

SWANSEA LIBRARIES

0001279420

© 2010 Playstage
An imprint of Write Publications Ltd.

All rights pertaining to this play or any part of this play are the property of the author
and managed by Playstage, PO Box 52, AXMINSTER, EX13 5WB, United Kingdom.
Licences to perform this play are issued by Playstage upon payment of a fee. To give a
reading or performance of this play without possession of a licence issued by Playstage
is an infringement of copyright.

PLEASE CHECK THAT THIS PLAY IS AVAILABLE FOR PERFORMANCE BEFORE
COMMENCING REHEARSALS.

This play is protected under the Copyright Laws currently existing in every country
throughout the world. All rights pertaining to stage; motion picture; radio; audio; digi-
tal; television; public reading and translation into foreign languages are the property of
the author and his or her agents. No part of this play may be copied or stored in any
format without permission from the copyright holders. No part of this play may be al-
tered in any way without permission from the copyright holders.

Designed by Kate Lowe, Greensands Graphics
Printed by Creeds Ltd, Bridport, Dorset

Note to producers about staging "The Haunted Bookshop"

The book, by Christopher Morley, is one of those forgotten gems that was written in 1919. It is very much in the mould of John Buchan and Erskine Childers in that it deals with the uncertainty that followed the First World War and the feeling that Germany, although vanquished, was still hankering after world domination. What separates "The Haunted Bookshop" from other novels of the period is its lovable eccentricity, therefore, it should be played with a certain amount of "Boy's Own Adventure" gusto.

The original book was sent in America, in the district of Brooklyn, New York. However, we have set the play in England, in the district of Hampstead, London but it could, just as easily be set in any major city – Edinburgh, Paris, Brussels, Toronto, New York – on the Allied side of the Great War. Drama groups are given permission to make the necessary changes in the text without having to contact the publisher.

THE CHARACTERS

ROGER MIFFLIN is the eccentric second-hand bookshop proprietor whose passion for literature infuses everything that he does or says. He is friendly, if a little vague.

HELEN MIFFLIN is ROGER's wife. Sensible and practical, she nevertheless adores her eccentric husband and, whilst she throws her hands up in despair at some of his obsessions, she enjoys her life with him.

AUBREY GILBERT, in his thirties, is a survivor of the Great War, where he worked in intelligence. But, like all the men who returned, he is finding it hard to adjust to life after the war. He has taken a job in the newly-burgeoning industry of advertising and is doing his best to make a go of it but, as we see in the opening of the play, he is finding it difficult.

TITANIA CHAPMAN is in her late twenties and the pampered daughter of a wealthy food manufacturer. Her mother is worried about her daughter's lack of purpose and arranges for her to have a job at the bookstore. TITANIA is a good-natured and conscientious woman, who tries really hard to embrace the role of a bookseller's assistant.

MRS CHAPMAN is TITANIA's mother and an ardent booklover. She regularly attends ROGER MIFFLIN's Book Club, along with several other bibliophiles, MRS QUINCY, MR GLADFIST and MR BENSON. They are all passionate about books and have frequent arguments.

MRS STEINER is a mystery. She is employed as the Mifflin's cleaner. She is quiet, reserved and rather disapproving of everything. She does not speak with a German accent but exclaims in German when she has an accident.

MR STEINER is her taciturn husband, who is the thug of the conspiracy ring. Could be doubled by an actor who plays a member of the Bibliophile Club. He does not speak with a German accent either.

MR WEINTRAUB, the local chemist, *does* speak with a German accent. He is a stern man with no sense of humour.

POLICE INSPECTOR
His purpose really is to be involved the outcome of the plot at the end. It is a minor part but an important one. It could, obviously, be played by a member of the Bibliophile Club doubling up.

THE COSTUMES

1919, the year in which the play is set (and the year is important to the plot) was a period when people were coming out of Edwardian fashions but were not quite in the "flapper" era of the 1920's. Women wore their skirts/dresses just above the ankle; they had abandoned corsets in favour of liberty bodices so everything had a "straight up and down" appearance; and they had begun to crop their hair or wear long hair in two braids wound around their ears, like earphones. Jaunty little hats were preferred, like little turbans with small feathers. The big hats of the Edwardian era had gone but they were not yet into the cloche hats and headbands of the mid-1920s. Men's fashions changed very little between 1900 and 1920. Suits with waistcoats and shirts with stiff collars were worn. Large overcoats were important and bowler hats were preferred, in England, over trilbies or homburgs. Straw hats, blazers and flannels would be worn in summer but this play is set in winter. For research purposes we recommend the following websites:
www.fashionera.com/C20th_costume_history/1918_silhouettes_1.htm
www.marquise.de/en/1900/pics/1910/1910c.shtml
www.costumes.org/history/100pages/1920royaltailors.htm

THE SET

See SET PLAN at the back of the book. It is one set, which is split into the bookshop and the MIFFLIN's downstairs parlour. The two halves are divided by a partial wall and an opening with a curtain. It is important to the plot that there is a sash window stage left; an opening from the parlour to an alluded "upstairs"; and a bookshop door which has a glass panel in the top, with an old fashioned doorbell above. For research purposes we suggest you look at the period doorbells on the following website: www.doorchimesuk.co.uk It is also necessary to have an old fashioned candlestick telephone on the desk. For the bookshelves in the bookshop, it is important that the front, stage right, bookshelf has removable books and that they should look suitably old. It is a second-hand bookshop. Also, books of the period tended to be hardback books, in plain colours, with no dust jackets. There were no paperbacks, as such. For the other bookshelves, we recommend that you consider this website, which sells pre-formed plastic rows of books that can be affixed to flats and painted. The company produces a catalogue. www.peterevansstudios.co.uk

TECHNICAL REQUIREMENTS

It is essential to the plot that side lighting, suggesting moonlight, should be arranged to come through the front door of the bookshop and the window in the downstairs parlour when the rest of the stage is dark. Other lighting should be soft – from oil lamps in the parlour (optional) and electric light in the bookshop.

Gunshots are required in the second Act. Also, a large offstage explosion is required, with a big flash of light, when the bomb explodes in the backyard. Old fashioned police and ambulance bells are heard during the second act, after the explosion.

MUSIC

Between the scenes music should be of the period – perhaps a Palm Court Orchestra type of sound or popular songs of the period, but not War songs. Research on Amazon should yield some ideas.

THE HAUNTED BOOKSHOP

CAST

ROGER MIFFLIN	Eccentric owner of the Haunted Bookshop, aged 50 – 60.
AUBREY GILBERT	Earnest man, trying to make a career in advertising, aged early 30s.
HELEN MIFFLIN	Long-suffering but cheerful wife of ROGER, aged 50 – 60.
MRS STEINER	Uncommunicative cleaning lady, aged 40+.
MRS CHAPMAN	Jolly wife of a wealthy food manufacturer. Ardent member of ROGER's Bibliophile Club. Aged 50+

THE BIBLIOPHILES

MR GLADFIST*	Any age.
MR BENSON*	Any age.
MRS QUINCY	Any age.

MR STEINER*	The taciturn husband of MRS STEINER. Aged 40+
MR WEINTRAUB	Dour German. Local chemist. Aged 50 - 60.
TITANIA CHAPMAN	Daughter of Mrs Chapman. Rich girl, never had a job before but willing to do her best. Aged 25+
POLICE INSPECTOR*	Any age up to 60.

denotes parts that could be doubled.

5 males (with doubling), 5 females.

The action takes place in the bookshop and downstairs parlour of ROGER MIFFLIN's bookshop/home in Hampstead, London in January 1919.

THE HAUNTED BOOKSHOP
ACT 1.
SCENE 1.

The interior of the MIFFLIN's bookshop and their downstairs parlour. The bookshop consists of the front door, stage right, which has a glass top, on which is hanging a sign, facing out to the street. The side facing the audience says "THE HAUNTED BOOKSHOP IS NOW CLOSED". There is a freestanding bookcase just by the door (SEE SET PLAN) and further bookshelves along the back of the shop. Centre back is a small desk and chairs. Slightly off centre stage is a partial wall with a curtained opening leading to a small parlour, which has two armchairs and a low table between them. Behind the armchairs is an opening which leads to the "upstairs" of the building. In the stage left wall is a large sash window.

ROGER MIFFLIN is sitting at his desk in the centre of the bookshop. There are piles of books on top of the desk; a candlestick telephone; a metal cash box; pad and pencils. There is a cork notice board behind the desk with various bits of paper and card stuck to it. He is reading a book and he has a pencil stuck behind one ear. He is wearing a velvet smoking jacket, cravat and smoking cap (like a soft, embroidered fez). There is an armchair next to the front door and a couple of wooden chairs dotted around. MRS STEINER is cleaning, unseen, behind the bookshelves and she suddenly makes a clatter and startles ROGER.

ROGER   Good gracious, Mrs Steiner! Are you still here?

      (MRS STEINER (MRS S) appears from behind the bookshelves with a bucket of water and a cloth. She does not smile.)

MRS S   Yes, Mr Mifflin. The books are particularly dusty today.

ROGER   Ah, yes, they do tend to get that way in winter. It's because all the customers bring in the dust of their coal fires on their clothes and it settles on the books.

MRS S   Yes, sir.

ROGER   Now, Mrs Steiner, I have a fancy to read aloud and I'm not sure that you will want to be my audience. So I suggest that you finish up and go home, otherwise your ears may be assaulted by some unwelcome literary prose.

MR S   I shall go immediately sir.

             (MRS S hurriedly goes through the curtain into the parlour and disappears "upstairs" with the bucket and cloth. ROGER settles down to reading aloud.)

ROGER   *(reading)* Far be it from me to assert what everybody says must be true. Everybody is, often, as likely to be wrong as right. In the general experience, everybody has been wrong so often, and it has taken in most instances such a weary while to find out how wrong, that authority may prove to be fallible. Everybody may sometimes be right; "but that's no rule," as the ghost of Giles Scroggins says in the ballad. The dread word GHOST recalls me. Everybody said he looked like a haunted man….

             (MRS S reappears, with her coat and hat on, and ROGER stops reading. She glares at him and scuttles across the stage. Then looks back at him and tuts, before leaving through the front door. ROGER shrugs and resumes.)

             …The extent of my present claim for everybody is that they were, so far, right. He did.

Who could have seen his hollow cheek, his sunken, brilliant eye; his black-attired figure, indefinably grim, although well knit and well-proportioned; his grizzled hair hanging, like tangled seaweed about his face – as if he had been, through his whole life, a lonely mark for the chafing and beating of the great deep of humanity – but might have said that he looked like a haunted man?

(AUBREY GILBERT is seen, outside the door, looking at the sign. He then enters the shop and we see that the side of the sign, facing the street, reads, "THE HAUNTED BOOKSHOP IS NOW OPEN". Although the bell rings, ROGER is so caught up in his reading aloud that he does not hear it. AUBREY stands, listening, and looking a little bewildered.)

Who could have observed his manner, taciturn, thoughtful, gloomy, shadowed by habitual reserve, retiring always and jocund never, with a distraught air of reverting to a bygone place and time, or of listening to some old echoes in his mind, but might have said it was the manner of a haunted man? *(He puts the book down with a sigh of satisfaction)* Who indeed? What a splendid description!

(AUBREY coughs and startles ROGER)

Bless my soul! Have you been there all the time?

AUBREY   No, I don't think so. Only for the last bit, I think.

ROGER   Is there something I can help you with?

AUBREY   The name of this book shop – The Haunted Bookshop – it made me stop and look. I just wondered if this book shop was really haunted. Are you the proprietor?

ROGER	I am. Roger Mifflin is the name. Bookselling is my game. *(he stands and shakes AUBREY's hand)* How apt that you should come in as I was reading from Dickens' story The Haunted Man. Was the book calling to you?
AUBREY	No…I don't think so.
ROGER	Ah…but you never know. Have you ever noticed how some books track you down and hunt you out? It's one of the uncanniest things I know to follow a real book on its career – it follows you and follows you and drives you into a corner and makes you read it. Words can't describe the cunning of some books.
AUBREY	Er…I suppose. I've never really thought about it. I came in here to ask if you were the proprietor and…*(he produces a card for ROGER, who takes it)* I wanted to discuss with you the advisability of your letting us handle your advertising account, prepare snappy copy for you, and place it in large circulation mediums. Now the war's over, you ought to prepare some constructive campaign for bigger business.
ROGER	*(looking at the card)* Mm. Mr Aubrey Gilbert., the Grey Matter Advertising Agency. A very nice name, Aubrey Gilbert. A literary name, I feel. I could certainly do business with a man who had such a literary name but I'm afraid, old chap, I don't do any advertising of any kind.
AUBREY	*(aghast)* No advertising at all!
ROGER	Not in the sense that you mean. Such advertising as benefits me most is done for me by the snappiest copywriters in the business.

AUBREY	*(disappointed)* I suppose you mean Whitewash and Gilt?
ROGER	Not at all. The people who are doing my advertising are Stevenson, Browning, Conrad and Company.
AUBREY	Dear me, I don't know that agency at all. Still I doubt that their advertising copy has more pep than ours.
ROGER	I don't think you get me. I mean that my advertising is done by the books I sell. If I sell a man a book by Stevenson or Conrad, a book that delights or terrifies him, that man and that book become my living advertisements.
AUBREY	But that word of mouth advertising is exploded. You can't get distribution that way. You've got to keep your trademark before the public.
ROGER	By the bones of Schiller! Look here! You wouldn't go to a doctor, a medical specialist, and tell him he ought to advertise in papers and magazines? A doctor is advertised by the bodies he cures. My business is advertised by the minds I stimulate. And let me tell you that the book business is different from other trades. People don't *know* that they want books. I can just by looking at you that your mind is ill for lack of books but you are blissfully unaware of it!
AUBREY	*(confused)* I am?
ROGER	Yes, yes. Sit down dear chap. *(He propels AUBREY into the arm chair)* People don't go to a bookseller until some serious mental accident or disease makes them aware of their danger. Then they come here. For me to advertise would be about as useful as telling people who feel perfectly well that they ought to go to a doctor. Do you know why people are reading more books now than ever before?

AUBREY   No.

ROGER   Because the terrible catastrophe of the war has made them
             realise that their minds are ill. The world was suffering all
             sorts of mental fevers and aches and disorders, and never
             knew it. Now our mental pangs are only too manifest. We
             are all reading hungrily, hastily, trying to find out…after the
             trouble is over…what was the matter with our minds.

AUBREY   You don't say.

ROGER   I do say! People *need* books, but they don't know that they
             need them. Generally, they are not aware that the books that
             they need are in existence.

AUBREY   But wouldn't advertising be the way to let them know?

ROGER   My dear chap, I understand the value of advertising. But in
             my own case it would be futile. I am not a dealer in
             merchandise but a specialist in adjusting the book to the
             human need. Between ourselves, there is no such thing as a
             "good" book. A book is only good when it meets some
             human hunger or refutes some human error. A book that is
             very good for me would very likely be useless to you. My
             pleasure is to prescribe books for such patients as drop in
             here and are willing to tell me their symptoms. Most are still
             open to treatment. There are, of course, those unfortunate
             souls who have let their reading faculties decay to such an
             extent that all I can do is hold a post mortem on them but
             most can be saved. There is no one as grateful as the man, or
             woman, to whom you have given just the book that his or
             her soul needed.

AUBREY   I should like to come here myself and browse about. I think
             I should like to have you prescribe for me. Are you open late?

ROGER	I stay open every evening until ten p.m. A great many of my customers work all day and can only visit a bookshop at night. The real book lovers, you know, are generally amongst the humbler classes.
	(Mr WEINTRAUB (MR. W) enters the shop. He is carrying a paper bag containing a bottle of sleeping medicine.)
	Ah! Mr Weintraub! *(To AUBREY)* Excuse me Mr.Gilbert. *(He goes over to MR.W)* How can I help you sir?
MR.W	*(speaks with a German accent)* I brought your wife's sleep medication. She ordered it yesterday.
ROGER	Oh there was no need to deliver it, Mr Weintraub. Goodness, you are only in the next street! I could have picked it up!
MR. W	*(handing it over)* It was no trouble. I wanted a book anyway.
ROGER	*(beaming)* Oh really? I'm afraid we don't have much in German, you know…
MR. W	No, no. I want a book in English. Carlyle's Oliver Cromwell.
ROGER	Oh. *(he looks at MR. W with concern)* Are you sure?
MR. W	There is a problem?
ROGER	No…well, yes. I don't see the book appealing to you, that's all. It is apparently, the Prime Minister's favourite book – but then that is understandable. Mr Lloyd George is, after all, a radical, of sorts, and would appreciate the life story of Oliver Cromwell…but, for you, I would have recommended… The Morte D'Arthur by Sir Thomas Malory. A bit of chivalry and romance, you know.

MR. W	*(irritable)* I wish to purchase Carlyle's Cromwell. Is there a problem? I could always get it somewhere else.
ROGER	No, no. It's right here. *(he goes to the first bookshelf and scans it)* Well, that's odd! It was here! I can't think what can have become of it! My apologies Mr Weintraub. I shall search for it and send it round to you.
MR. W	No, don't bother. I need the book quickly. I shall try elsewhere.
ROGER	Oh dear. I'm sorry not to have been able to help you. What do I owe you for the medicine?
MR.W	Nothing. Your wife already paid. Good day, sir. (MR.W. leaves)
ROGER	*(looking after him and shaking his head, then turning to AUBREY)* Now there is a classic example of someone who doesn't know what book he should really have and refuses to take advice. I'm afraid Carlyle's Cromwell is going to give him terrible indigestion.
AUBREY	Strange choice of book for a German.
ROGER	Ah yes. Poor man. He has been in this country for years and he didn't take too kindly to being interned as an enemy alien for the duration of the war, I can tell you. He should be reading books filled with hope and joy – otherwise he will never get himself out of his melancholy.
AUBREY	Changing the subject, Mr Mifflin, I don't suppose you know of any lodgings around here, do you? Only, I have been given this area of North London as my patch and I feel I must move from my present accommodation.
ROGER	As a matter of fact I do. Mrs Smith, just over the road, has

rooms to rent. Very reasonable too, I'm told. *(having an idea)* Look here! Why don't you stay for supper? I'm all on my own this evening. My wife has gone to visit her sister in Surrey and won't be back until nearly midnight. I hate eating alone. So why don't you stay and have a bite with me? Then I'll take you over and introduce you to Mrs Smith. What do you say?

AUBREY   I say, that's jolly decent of you. Are you sure you don't mind?

ROGER   Not at all. Please come through to my little parlour.

(ROGER hustles AUBREY through to the parlour and sits him in one of the two armchairs. There is a newspaper on the low table between the chairs.)

Now you have a sit down here and read the newspaper while I prepare the food. I'm afraid it will have to be cheese on toast. I can't muster anything better when Mrs Mifflin is away. She's the cook in this household.

AUBREY   *(smiling)* Do you know, I was just thinking about how much I should enjoy a bit of cheese on toast as I was walking down the street. Cheese on toast is my favourite food.

ROGER   *(beaming)* Excellent! Oh, and my apologies about having to eat down here but I have to be available in case a customer comes in to the shop.

AUBREY   That's absolutely fine.

ROGER   Good! Good! Well take your coat off, my dear chap, and make yourself comfortable. I shan't be long.

(ROGER goes "upstairs" and AUBREY takes his coat off and settles down to read the paper. After about thirty seconds, the telephone in the shop rings. AUBREY looks up from his paper and wonders what to do.)

ROGER	*(offstage)* Could you get that, dear chap? And take a message? There's a pad and pencils on the desk.
AUBREY	Righto! *(AUBREY goes and answers the telephone.)*

Hallo? Er…the Haunted Bookshop here. *(pause)* Who am I? Um…I'm Mr.Mifflin's assistant. Whom may I say is calling? *(pause) (a little tetchy)* Look here…madam…I apologise for being so blunt but, frankly, is it any of your business if Mr Mifflin wants to take on an assistant? *(pause, then he looks dismayed)* I say, I'm terribly sorry, Mrs Mifflin…of course it's your business…please allow me to explain…*(pause)* My name is Aubrey Gilbert and I represent The Grey Matter Advertising Agency. I just dropped in on the off-chance that your husband might want us to represent him and the next thing I know I'm being told I'm sick in the head for want of a good book and he invited me to supper…*(he holds the phone away from his ear as she is obviously being rather loud, then he speaks with some relief)* I'm so glad you find it humorous. *(pause)* Typical of him, is it? *(he nods as she speaks)* Right! Yes! Let me just get a pencil. *(he finds a pencil and some paper and with some difficulty he writes on a pad whilst holding the earpiece to his ear)* Yes, I'm ready. *(he listens and repeats what she says)* Can't get back tonight …sister not well…be back the day after tomorrow… chocolate cake in the pantry for the….sorry…didn't quite get that last word…*(he writes and speaks slowly)* bib..lee..o…files…is that right? Bibliophiles? *(pause)* Right. Nice to speak to you to, Mrs Mifflin. Goodbye. *(AUBREY tears off the sheet of paper and goes back to the parlour, he has just sat down when ROGER appears with two plates of toasted cheese.)*

ROGER	Was it anyone important?
AUBREY	Your wife. *(he hands ROGER the sheet of paper).*
ROGER cake in	*(reading)*…sister sick…back day after tomorrow…chocolate pantry…ah, well…as long as the cake is ready.
AUBREY	Who are the Bibliophiles?
ROGER	Ah. Let me get us a glass of beer to go with our cheese on toast and I'll tell you. *(AUBREY starts to eat his supper, whilst ROGER nips back "upstairs" and returns with two glasses of beer.)*
AUBREY	The cheese on toast is excellent. Just hits the spot. Hadn't realised how hungry I was.
ROGER	Good! Good! Here's your beer! *(he sits in the other armchair and holds up his glass towards AUBREY)* To new friends, eh?
AUBREY	*(clinking his glass to ROGER's)* New friends.
ROGER	Before I tell you about the Bibliophiles, tell me a little about yourself, Mr Gilbert…
AUBREY	Do call me Aubrey. When people call me Mr Gilbert, I keep thinking they are talking about my father.
ROGER	Aubrey. So what did you do in the war? Were you in the thick of it? *(ROGER eats while AUBREY talks)*
AUBREY	No, thank God. I felt guilty about that. I should have been but they put me in Army Intelligence. I never went anywhere near the front line.
ROGER	Army intelligence? They must have thought you had important skills.
AUBREY	Oh I don't know about that. I've always liked to do puzzles,

crosswords, that sort of thing and I suppose it helped that I spoke a bit of German. All the chaps in Intelligence seemed to be like me.

ROGER   Did anything exciting ever happen to you?

AUBREY   Not really...well...I suppose there was the Mata Hari thing...

ROGER   *(impressed)* You were involved with the famous spy Mata Hari?

AUBREY   Well, not personally, you understand. I just had to do some surveillance and some reports on her.

ROGER   Was she very beautiful?

AUBREY   Not really. I thought, personally, she was a bit dumpy. But she took her clothes off a lot – on stage – and I suppose that attracted a certain type of man. She was, supposedly, very good at the seductress bit. Silly woman, in my opinion. More foolish than calculating. They shouldn't have shot her. Don't hold with shooting women.

ROGER   No. And what about this advertising lark? How did you get into that?

AUBREY   Captain in my regiment. His father owns The Grey Matter Advertising Agency. Kindly gave me a job after the war. I've only been there since I was demobbed a couple of months ago.

ROGER   Do you like it?

AUBREY   Actually, it's not bad. I seem to be quite good at making up slogans and things. I've done quite well on one particular account – the Chapman Daintybits Company.

ROGER   *(astonished)* Well I'm blowed! What a small world!

AUBREY   You know him? Mr Chapman?

ROGER   Well not him, personally, but his wife is a member of the
           Bibliophile Club.

AUBREY   *(enthusiastically)* There is a man – Chapman – who can tell
           you all about the virtues of advertising. We handle all his
           copy. We made Chapman prunes a staple of civilisation and
           culture. I devised the slogan "We preen ourselves on our
           prunes", which you see in every big magazine. Chapman
           prunes are known the world over. The Pope eats them. The
           Prime Minister eats them. In fact, we've just heard that
           thirteen cases of them are to be put aboard the Isle de France
           for Lloyd George's voyage to the Paris peace Conference.
           And the Czechoslovak Army were fed largely on prunes. It is
           our conviction in the office that Chapman prunes largely
           won the war.

ROGER   Really? I must try some.

AUBREY   Well, enough about me. Tell me about this Bibliophile Club
           of yours.

ROGER   Ah, yes. Well it's just a small gathering, really, of people who
           are either avid readers of books or enthusiastic booksellers.
           We have some lively discussions. You must come along.
           You'd enjoy it. Can you make tomorrow afternoon? I close
           early on Wednesdays and that is when we meet – here – in
           the bookshop.

AUBREY   I suppose so. Will it be my sort of thing, do you think? I
           mean I haven't had much time for reading in the last few
           years.

ROGER   It will be exactly your sort of thing. And that reminds me...
before I take you over to Mrs Smith's lodging house, I shall
prescribe a book. Now that I know you better, I know just
the book that you need. Come with me.

*(ROGER goes into the bookshop and AUBREY follows.
ROGER scans the shelves of the front bookcase and takes
out a book.)*

Ah! Here we are! It was waiting for you. Books, as I said
before, are remarkably cunning. This one knew it was
destined for you, the moment you walked into the shop, so
it has been glowing a little brighter so that I could find it
easily. Here we are, Sir Walter Scott's Ivanhoe. A tale of a
heroic Englishman who rescues beautiful women. Tailor
made for you. I take it you haven't read it?

AUBREY   No. I've heard of it, though. You're right, it does sound like
a book I would enjoy. You're rather skilled at this book-
prescribing aren't you?

ROGER   A man should always build on his strengths. Matching
books with people is mine.

AUBREY   Thank you very much, Mr Mifflin.

ROGER   Roger, please. Now, if you would like to get your coat, we
shall go over and meet the redoubtable Mrs Smith. Don't be
put off by her yappy dog. It makes a lot of noise but it
wouldn't hurt a fly.

AUBREY   Righto.

*(AUBREY goes back to the parlour and gets his coat and
briefcase, whilst ROGER waits for him at the door.)*

You never did tell me why you call this shop The Haunted
Bookshop. Is it haunted?

ROGER	You know, I'm not really sure. I think it may be haunted by the ghosts of all those writers who truly want to be read. There are some writers who only write for themselves, of course, and everyone else finds them unreadable. But I think the ones who really want to be read sort of linger about their books and urge readers forward. It can get quite lively in here.
AUBREY	I should have thought that living in a bookshop would be delightfully tranquil.
ROGER	Far from it, my dear chap! Living in a bookshop is like living in a warehouse of explosives. Those shelves are ranked with the most furious combustibles in the world – the brains of men. I can spend a rainy afternoon reading and my mind works itself up to such a passion and anxiety over mortal problems as almost unmans me. It is terribly nerve-wracking. Surround a man with Carlyle, Emerson, Thoreau, Chesterton, Shaw, Nietzsche and would you wonder at his getting excited? It's like being a cat living in a room wallpapered with catnip!
AUBREY	How is it, though, that libraries are shrines of such austere calm? If books are as provocative as you suggest, one would expect every librarian one meets to be hysterical.
ROGER	Ah, my boy, you forget the card index! Librarians invented that soothing device to calm their souls. Librarians would, indeed, go mad, if they did not have the cool and healing card index to fall back on.
AUBREY	I'd never thought of that. A bit like smoking a pipe in times of stress, I suppose.
ROGER	Exactly. Now shall we adjourn to Mrs Smith's?

AUBREY   Yes, of course.

ROGER   And, don't forget…the Bibliophile Club meets here
              tomorrow at two thirty in the afternoon.

AUBREY   I shall be here.

              (ROGER turns the sign around on the door so that it reads
              "THE HAUNTED BOOKSHOP IS NOW CLOSED" and
              they both exit.)

Lights fade to black.

Music.

End of SCENE 1.

THE HAUNTED BOOKSHOP

ACT 1

SCENE 2

*In the bookshop. The lights go up to the sound of The Bibliophile Club
arguing strenuously. Every available chair is gathered in the middle of the
bookshop and seated is MRS CHAPMAN (MRS C.), wearing an elegant dress
and hat with a fur wrap, MRS QUINCY, MR GLADFIST, and MR
BENSON. AUBREY is seated against the stage left "wall", with a briefcase
next to his chair, and ROGER is standing.*

QUINCY	…it was not at all a suitable book, I tell you…
GLADFIST	So you say!
BENSON	I don't believe you bothered to read it….
QUINCY	Well, there's no need to be rude!
ROGER	Gentlemen! Ladies! Calm yourselves, please!
	(There is silence and ROGER looks relieved)
	I know that our passions sometimes run away with us in this club but, really! I've never known such excitement about a book before.
QUINCY	Well, I'm sorry but, in my opinion, The Rainbow by D.H Lawrence should be banned. It's filth. Pure filth. And the awful man is married to Baron von Richthoven's sister! Any book by him should be banned on two counts – pornography and treason.

ROGER   Well. I can see that one should be very careful when introducing new books to members of the fairer sex. My dear lady, I do apologise. How did *you* find the book, Mrs Chapman?

MRS C   I have to confess that I threw the towel in after the first chapter. It was all a bit too racy for me and – to be honest – there wasn't much of a plot, I thought.

BENSON   *(grudgingly)* Well, true. I'll give you that.

GLADFIST   But look here, times have changed, you know. All these emancipated women and the such like. One shouldn't throw out modern novels because they cross some boundaries. I mean, even some of the old novels are a bit…well…you know. Take Emile Zola, for instance.

QUINCY   *(making a noise of disgust)* Well what can you expect from the French? They're obsessed with sex. You don't get any of that sort of stuff in a good British novel – Rudyard Kipling; Sir Arthur Conan Doyle; Erskine Childers – all books I would give to my grandmother to read.

AUBREY   *(suddenly chipping in)* Tarzan Of The Apes is on at the cinema. Is anyone going to see it?

(They all turn round and look at him. There is a pause. Everyone looks astonished except MRS CHAPMAN who smiles.)

ROGER   Not while I can read The Jungle Book. I've never seen the point of these silent films. A lot of dumb show and then you have to read the captions. But it's an American invention and I suppose just one step up from reading comics. In my opinion, it encourages illiteracy.

BENSON	How can it encourage illiteracy, if you have to read the captions?
ROGER	Well you could go to the cinema with a friend who could read the captions for you, I suppose.
GLADFIST	You make me tired with all your talk of literature. A book's a book if you enjoy reading it. Lots of people enjoy pulp fiction. I know it's tripe and it would probably kill *me* to read it but let's be tolerant.
MRS C	*(to AUBREY)* My daughter is certainly a fan of the cinema. It's a young person's thing I suppose. What is it exactly that you enjoy about it, young man?
AUBREY	Well…it's modern. I suppose it's just that it's something different, that's all.
ROGER	But it's silent. One might as well go and see a good play.
AUBREY	True. I don't know, to be honest.
BENSON	It's none of our business to say what's good and what isn't. As booksellers, our job is simply to supply the public with the books it wants, when it wants them. How it comes to want those books is no concern of ours. Although I will say that if people go and watch a film at the cinema and it stimulates them to come into my shop and buy the book of Tarzan, then I'm not going to complain.
ROGER	*(annoyed)* You're the chap who usually calls bookselling the worst business in the world and you're the kind of chap who makes it so. I suppose you would say that it is no concern of the bookseller to try and increase the public appetite for decent literature?
BENSON	Appetite is too strong a word. As far as literature is

concerned the public is barely able to sit up and take a little liquid nourishment. The solid food of high-minded literature doesn't interest the public. If you try and cram roast beef down the gullet of an invalid, you'll kill him. Let the public alone, is what I say, and thank God when it comes round to spend some of its hard-earned cash on pulp fiction.

ROGER *(hotly)* Well, I'd like to bet that the trade has made more money from Jane Austen than all the Tarzan books put together.

BENSON *(forcefully)* What of it? Why shouldn't we make money from both?

QUINCY Gentlemen, gentlemen! There's no need to get hot under the collar!

MRS C Time for some refreshment, I think, Mr Mifflin! No doubt your wife has baked her usual delicious cake?

ROGER She has indeed, I'll call Mrs Steiner. *(He goes into the parlour and calls up the "stairs".)* Mrs Steiner! Could you bring the refreshments, please?

(Everyone gets up and stretches their legs. GLADFIST, QUINCY and BENSON go into a huddle. ROGER joins them but MR C comes over to AUBREY)

MRS C Well! You certainly opened up and avenue of discussion, young man!

AUBREY I'm awfully sorry.

MRS C No! Don't apologise! The Bibliophile Club thrives on heated argument. It's the reason I come. Being married to a most reasonable man, I realised that a good, hearty disagreement was something sadly lacking in my life. So I jumped at the chance to join Mr Mifflin's little club. Every week I go home thoroughly invigorated! But tell me – why have *you* joined?

AUBREY   By chance really. I came into Mr Mifflin's shop to ask whether he would like to be represented by our advertising agency and the next thing I found was that I was living opposite and being prescribed Ivanhoe to read.

MRS C   *(laughing)* That sounds like Mr Mifflin's tactics! What advertising agency do you represent...Mr...?

AUBREY   *(shaking her hand)* I'm sorry. How rude of me. The name's Aubrey Gilbert. I work for the Grey Matter Advertising Agency.

MRS C   Oh! Well, then you must know my husband – Oliver Chapman, of ChapmansDaintybits Food Company?

AUBREY   I should say I do! Well, I don't know him personally, but in the last two months I've worked extensively on the Chapman campaign.

MRS C   Have you? Then you must be doing a good job because he's very pleased with it.

(A grim-faced MRS STEINER appears with glasses of cider, a chocolate cake, some cloth napkins, forks, small plates and a cake knife on a tray. She dumps them down on the desk, glares at ROGER and then goes back upstairs.)

QUINCY   I see the redoubtable Mrs Steiner is still tyrannising this shop.

ROGER   Ssh! Or she'll hear you!

MRS C   *(to AUBREY)* Come and get some refreshment, Mr Gilbert, and you can tell me more about yourself.

(*MRS C and AUBREY drift over to the refreshments. ROGER is cutting the cake, putting pieces on plates. People take a plate of cake, a fork and a napkin and resume their conversations.*)

ROGER   (*To QUINCY*) I keep Mrs Steiner on because I feel the woman is a soul in torment. In need of a good book, you understand. One that will break her reserve and re-introduce her to the human race. I keep trying to tempt her but I've had no luck so far.

QUINCY   I should give up if I were you. Some people are beyond redemption.

ROGER   You may be right.

GLADFIST   (*to BENSON*) You see, you must select your stock according to your customers. Would there be any point in filling up your shelves with Homer and Thackeray when the public wants Edgar Wallace thrillers and penny romances? I mean, does a country grocer carry the same cigars listed on the wine card at the Savoy? Of course not. He gets in the cigars that his trade enjoys and is accustomed to. Bookselling must obey the rules of ordinary commerce.

ROGER   (*overhearing*) I don't give a fig for the ordinary rules of commerce! I moved to Hampstead to get away from them. My mind would blow its fuses if I had to abide by the dirty little considerations of supply and demand. As far as I'm concerned, supply creates demand.

GLADFIST   Still, old chap, you have to abide by the dirty little consideration of earning a living, don't you? Unless you are independently wealthy, of course.

BENSON   You have to listen to him, Mifflin. Take it from me, folks
            will pay a darn sight more to be amused than they will to be
            improved. Look at what they charge for cinema tickets or
            theatre tickets! *(to AUBREY)* How much are cinema tickets,
            by the way, sir?

AUBREY   Three and sixpence, last time I looked.

ROGER   *(aghast)* Three and sixpence!? I could buy three volumes of
            poetry for that!

BENSON   My point exactly. A man will shell out, God knows what,
            for cinema tickets to impress a girl – but would he spend
            that money on books so as he could read her poetry? Not at
            all!

GLADFIST   The mistake that we, in the booktrade have made, is trying
            to tell people that books are necessities. Tell them that they
            are luxuries and they'll be queuing up to buy 'em. People
            work so hard in this life – and there's the hangover from the
            war to consider – that a chap will let his suit become
            threadbare rather than go without the best cigar or the finest
            malt whisky.

BENSON   Exactly. In fact I think it is more charitable not to take
            advantage of the gullible public when they come into a
            bookshop and don't know what they want. Rather than
            trying to ram some shimmering stuff at them just because
            they ought to read it, I say let the poor boobs blunder
            around and grab what takes their fancy! Let natural
            selection operate. I think it's fascinating to watch them, to
            see their helpless groping, and to study the weird ways in
            which they make their choice. Usually they will buy a book
            because they think the cover is attractive, or because it costs

one shilling instead of two, or because they saw a review of it. I don't think one book-buyer in a thousand knows what they are doing.

ROGER   *(appalled)* Your doctrine is pitiless, base and false! What would you think of a physician who saw men suffering from from a curable disease and did nothing to alleviate their sufferings?

GLADFIST   The sufferings, as you call them, are nothing to what mine would be if I stocked up with a lot of books that no-one but highbrows would buy. What would you think of a base public that would go past my shop day after day and let the high-minded occupant die of starvation?

MRS C   Have we all finished refreshments? Because I think we should all sit down again. This argument is proving to be most challenging and I feel I could better contribute if I were seated.

ROGER   Of course, dear lady, of course. Shall we all be seated again?

(There is a flurry of returning plates and glasses and everyone resumes their seats.)

QUINCY   I should like to say that, as a mere reader and not a member of the booktrade, I value the input of a good bookseller. I mean if I may go back to the hideous D.H Lawrence book I spoke about earlier, I should like to think that a good bookseller would steer young and impressionable minds away from such books – or perhaps even not stock them at all!

ROGER   Hear, hear!

GLADFIST   But it all comes down to public taste again. If there is a demand for such books, then we have to stock them.

Personally, I keep them in a section marked "For adult consumption only" which keeps all the ladies of delicate sensibilities away.

MRS C   But surely the original fault lies with the publishers? Most of them don't seem to know a good book when they see it. My husband's company, which deals in foodstuffs, spends vast sums of money on chemically assaying and analysing the ingredients that are to go into his foods. And yet, they tell me that the most important department of a publishing business, which is the gathering and sampling of manuscripts, is the least considered and the worst paid in the company! I knew a reader for one publishing house – a young man recently out of college – who, frankly, didn't know a good book from a handkerchief! Now, if my husband's company can employ a trained chemist to select ingredients for his foodstuffs, why can't a publishing company employ expert book analysers?

(There is a general hubbub of people agreeing and disagreeing.)

ROGER   Do you know, Mrs Chapman, I think you may have something there. Now, we might write to the various publishing houses, as a group – namely, The Bibliophile Club, and ask if our views might be included in their selection processes.

GLADFIST   Would there be any money in it for us though? I'm sorry to raise the spectre of filthy lucre again but one has to make a living.

ROGER   Well we might mention that, for a small fee, we could read and assess manuscripts for them. What do you think?

(General hubbub of agreement)

ROGER   And this brings me nicely on to sharing with you a long-held
             dream of mine – the bookshop on wheels...

QUINCY   I beg your pardon, Mr Mifflin...did you say "a bookshop on
             wheels"?

ROGER   I did indeed, Mrs Quincy. I have long felt that people who
             live outside of this great metropolis, or indeed any other
             metropolis such as Manchester or Edinburgh, have very little
             access to books. They can, of course, order them by post but
             they are lacking any opportunity to browse. Even if they
             want to go to a library, they have to go to a city and,
             obviously, that limits their time. Think of it! *(he gets very
             enthusiastic)* A fleet of motorised bookshops that would
             take an eclectic mix of stock out to the rural populace of
             Great Britain!

MRS C   What a splendid idea!

AUBREY   I bet you could buy up some Army vehicles really cheaply.
             They won't have much use for them now.

GLADFIST   Not a bad idea. It's something that the cinema is doing, of
             course. The projectionist and his equipment travelling
             around and showing films in the villages.

BENSON   Bet it would cost a pretty penny though.

ROGER   True. I had only thought of what a contribution the scheme
             would make to the world's happiness. Books are the
             depositories of the human spirit, which is the only thing in
             the world that endures. What was it Shakespeare said?
             Not marble nor the gilded monuments
             Of princes shall outlive this powerful rhyme –

(MRS STEINER comes in quietly and starts to put plates etc. On the tray. She looks up suddenly when ROGER says…)

And he was right. And there's something in Carlyle's Cromwell about it too – if only I could find the blessed book.

MRS C   *(reaching in to her handbag)* Oh, you lent it to me, Mr Mifflin! Don't you remember? *(she hands ROGER the book and MRS STEINER watches carefully).*

ROGER   Bless my soul! So I did!

GLADFIST   What *is* it about that book at the moment? I had some chap come in and ask for it yesterday and to my dismay I didn't have a copy in stock.

BENSON   Yes I had someone come in and ask for it too! I don't think I've ever been asked for that book before, so, of course, I didn't have it in stock either.

QUINCY   Perhaps someone's been advertising it somewhere, hence the public interest.

GLADFIST   *(to BENSON)* Was your chap German?

BENSON   Yes, I believe he was! Rum looking cove. Looked like a smile would kill him.

GLADFIST   It's the same chap. There's no public demand then. Just one odd-looking German wanting the same book.

ROGER   Oh that'll be Mr Weintraub. He owns a chemist's shop round the corner. He came in here looking for the book and I couldn't find it. I'll take it round to him tomorrow.

(MRS STEINER exits with the tray).

QUINCY	Well, I must be going now, Mr Mifflin. Thank your wife for the lovely cake. *(QUINCY gets up and so do the others.)*
GLADFIST	I must be making tracks too. *(shaking ROGER's hand)* Thank you Mifflin for the usual stimulating meeting.
BENSON	*(also shakes ROGER's hand)* Yes, capital as usual, old chap.
	(They leave. ROGER puts the book on the desk.)
MRS C	Mr Mifflin? Do you think I might have a quick word?
ROGER	*(coming over to her)* Of course, Mrs Chapman.
AUBREY	Well, I'd best be leaving too…
MRS C	Oh no! Do stay just a little, Mr Gilbert. I should like to talk to you as well.
AUBREY	*(Intrigued)* Righto. *(he leaves his briefcase about two feet from the front door and comes over to MRS C and ROGER)*
MRS C	Well now, Mr Mifflin. As you know, I have a daughter – Titania. A charming girl, if only we could get some of the finishing school nonsense out of her head. She's had the advantage, you see, of having every possible want and whim gratified throughout her life and her father and I, out of kindness for herself and her future husband, if she should have one, want her to learn a little about earning a living. We've told her that if she would try to get a job for a while then we would take her to America at some stage. Now, this is my plan, if you would agree to it. We want her to think that she is really earning her way but we don't want you to be out of pocket for this little experiment. So my husband and I are proposing, if you are agreeable, that we should pay you three pounds a week if you would employ her and pay

her one pound and ten shillings out of that money, as her wage, and keep the rest for board and keep. I suppose you do have a room that she might use, do you? Otherwise I was wondering if there were any rooms for rent in Mr Gilbert's lodgings across the street?

ROGER   My dear lady! It would be an honour to take your daughter in to our home and shop. We have a perfectly excellent spare room upstairs, which could be made ready in an instant. I should greatly enjoy having an assistant to whom I could teach the joys of bookselling!

MRS C   And you, Mr Gilbert...I was wondering if you might show my daughter how she might spend her wages wisely each week in social pursuits, such as the cinema you mentioned. Would that be too great an imposition upon you? Only I do want Titania to learn how to earn and use money like ordinary people do.

          (MRS STEINER comes in quietly, at this point, with her hat and coat on. She goes to the desk and swiftly pockets the Cromwell book and then goes towards the door)

AUBREY   No...er...no imposition at all, Mrs Chapman.

MRS C   But you must understand, both of you, that I do not want Titania to know that we are supporting her financially in this endeavour – otherwise she will not make her best efforts.

ROGER   Of course.

AUBREY   Absolutely.

MRS C   Good. Then I shall send her over tomorrow.

MRS S   *(turning and facing the others)* Mr Mifflin, I am going now.

Will Mrs Mifflin be here tomorrow?

ROGER   I hope so, Mrs Steiner.

MRS S   Good. I have something important I want to talk to her about.

ROGER   I'll let her know.

(MRS STEINER turns to go but does not notice the briefcase which she trips over and it sends her sprawling to the floor)

MRS S   Gott in Himmel!

(Everyone reacts to her fall)

AUBREY   *(rushing towards her)* I'm most terribly sorry! Are you hurt?

MRS S   My ankle! Oh the pain!

MRS C   Oh dear me! The poor woman's injured herself quite badly!

AUBREY   Blast, it's all my fault! Let me help you on to a chair.

(AUBREY helps her on to the nearest chair. MRS STEINER is in a great deal of pain.)

MRS C   The poor woman needs to go to hospital. My chauffeur is sitting in my car opposite. Mr Gilbert, do you think you could help Mrs Steiner to my car and I'll take her to the casualty department?

AUBREY   Yes, of course.

MRS S   Aagh! My ankle is broken! Mr Mifflin, you will have to send a message to my husband!

ROGER   Yes, yes. Of course.

MRS C   Come along now, Mr Gilbert.

(MRS C holds the door open while AUBREY helps MRS S out of the shop.)

ROGER   *(to himself)* Right, I must get my coat and run these errands.
*(He goes into the parlour to fetch his jacket and scarf, which
are hanging on the hat stand in the parlour).*

Now. First to Mrs Steiner's flat and then I might as well
deliver the book to Mr Weintraub. *(he goes to the desk.)*
Gone again! Bless my soul, this book is certainly proving
elusive! *(he searches amongst the books and papers on the
desk and then gives up.)* No. It just won't be found!

(ROGER goes to the door and opens it, then pauses.)

I'm beginning to think that this book shop really is haunted!

(He closes the door and locks it with a key.)

FADE TO BLACK.

Music.

END OF SCENE 2.

THE HAUNTED BOOKSHOP

ACT 1.

SCENE 3.

The next afternoon. ROGER is standing by the half open door and calling to a customer who has just left the shop.

ROGER   …and don't forget, Mrs Harper, do sit down when you read that book. It's very moving and I wouldn't want you to feel giddy! *(He waves, then closes the door with a happy sigh and returns to his desk.)* Another prescription filled satisfactorily!

    (He returns to reading his book, only to be disturbed by AUBREY coming in to the shop, clutching a book.)

    Hallo, Aubrey! Have you finished Ivanhoe already?

AUBREY   I have – and jolly exciting it was too. All that dashing about and rescuing damsels. I quite worked up a sweat. I feel now, as though I am ready to purchase a book!

ROGER   *(beaming)* Splendid, splendid! Let's look at what's on offer shall we?

    (ROGER takes AUBREY behind the front bookshelf and we hear him muttering about books. HELEN enters through the front door, wearing her coat and hat and carrying a small suitcase.)

HELEN   Roger! Have you dozed off behind the book stacks again?

ROGER   *(emerging with AUBREY and flinging wide his arms)* My darling!

You've returned at last! *(He gives her a hug and a peck on the cheek. She smiles.)* We've had such larks here, while you've been away, haven't we, Aubrey? Oh, where are my manners? Aubrey Gilbert, this is my wife, Helen. Helen, this is the young man you spoke to on the phone, Mr Aubrey Gilbert.

(HELEN smiles and shakes AUBREY's hand.)

HELEN Ah! The informal "assistant"!

AUBREY Look here, Mrs Mifflin, I'm awfully sorry if I was a bit abrupt on the phone...

HELEN Oh pish! Think nothing of it, Mr Gilbert. I am only too well aware of the confusing effect that Roger has on people.

ROGER Oh...speaking of assistants....there's something I have to tell you...

HELEN Let me guess. You've let our spare room to Mr Gilbert, who is leaving advertising and going in to the book business...

ROGER Well, no...not quite. I don't quite know where to begin...

HELEN Well let me get my hat and coat off and sit down. I have a feeling that what you are about to tell me will be momentous. *(HELEN takes her suitcase into the parlour and removes her hat and coat, talking as she does so.)* By the way, my sister is now fine...thank you for asking. It was just a migraine, poor dear but I didn't like to leave her until it was over. I did stop by the Old Angle Bookshop yesterday, just to say hallo to Mr. Jillings. He says all booksellers are crazy but that you are the craziest of the lot. *(she re-appears from the parlour.)* He wants to know if you're bankrupt yet.

ROGER	*(chuckling)* And what did you say?
HELEN	I said that our bookshop was haunted and the usual conditions of trade didn't apply.
ROGER	Bully for you! And what did old Jillings say?
HELEN	He said, yes, haunted by a crazed bookseller who will go bankrupt any day now.
ROGER	Well, when literature goes bankrupt, I'm willing to go with it. Not till then. By the way, we are going to be haunted by a beauteous damsel today.
HELEN	Oh?
AUBREY	*(gloomily)* I bet she isn't beauteous.
ROGER	Mr and Mrs Chapman want to send their daughter to work in this shop and live with us, so that she will learn the value of hard work for little money. They are paying me so that I can pay her. But we must keep that bit quiet. Don't you think it will be rather interesting to get a naïve young girl's reaction towards the problem of our tranquil existence?
HELEN	Roger, you blessed innocent! Life will no longer be tranquil with a young girl around the place! You may fool yourself but you can't fool me. A girl of that age doesn't react towards things – she explodes! I suppose you know you're taking a human bombshell into the arsenal?
ROGER	*(looking doubtful)* I remember something in the book, Weir of Hermiston, about a girl being "an explosive engine" but I don't see she can do very much harm around here. The worst that could happen is if she got hold of my private copy of The Rainbow by D.H.Lawrence. Remind me to lock it up somewhere will you?

HELEN	And what is this creature's name?
AUBREY	Titania. And I bet she doesn't look like the Queen of the Fairies.
ROGER	Aubrey here is anxious about it all, since Mrs Chapman roped him in to squire Titania about when she is off-duty.
HELEN	*(laughing)* Poor you! I suspect you are right, Mr Gilbert. Girls with magical names rarely live up to them. Well, I'd better get Mrs Steiner to clean out the spare room…
ROGER	Ah. There's a small problem with that…
HELEN	*(suspiciously)* Explain yourself, Roger.
AUBREY	Look here, I'm awfully sorry. It was my fault. Left the blasted thing over there and she tripped. Came down a cropper, I'm afraid.
HELEN	Left what, where and is she still alive?
ROGER	Oh yes, she's still alive!
AUBREY	It was my briefcase, over by the door.
ROGER	She just has a bad ankle. Mrs Chapman took her to the hospital while I went to inform Mr Steiner that his wife had had an accident. We are awaiting progress reports.
HELEN	I can feel the benefit of my stay in the country dwindling away by the minute. So, no cleaning lady and an unexpected guest coming to stay. Any other little titbits you have yet to mention?
ROGER	No. I think that's it.
AUBREY	*(shaking his head)* No.
HELEN	Right, well I'd better roll my sleeves up and sort out this

spare room. If Titania arrives in the meantime, keep her amused until her living quarters are ready.

ROGER   Yes, dear.

HELEN   I would ask, Mr Gilbert, if you could you please keep my husband out of mischief – but I'm not altogether sure that you two aren't kindred spirits.

(HELEN sweeps out to the parlour and then "upstairs". ROGER and AUBREY look at each other sheepishly.)

AUBREY   In the doghouse, eh?

ROGER   Firmly, dear boy, firmly. But...I will say this about my wife...she is, in the main, a jolly soul and she doesn't harbour grudges. She'll be plying you with tea and sticky buns within the hour, I'm sure of it.

AUBREY   I'll take your word for it. I say, with reference to Mrs Steiner...did you notice that she swore in German when she tripped over my briefcase?

ROGER   I can't say that I did but I suppose with a name like Steiner, it's not unexpected.

AUBREY   Hmm. She doesn't speak with an accent though, does she?

ROGER   True.

AUBREY   You seem to be surrounded by Germans here. I should be careful if I were you. Can't trust the Boche one inch.

ROGER   My dear Aubrey! I hardly think one morose chemist and an unsociable cleaning lady are going to give me cause for concern! You must forget all that nationalistic nonsense now that the war is over, you know.

AUBREY   Sorry. You're right. My intelligence training is proving just a bit too hard to shake off.

*(The door opens and TITANIA enters. She is very nice
looking, wearing elegant clothes, a hat and a little fur collar.
She is carrying a small suitcase in one hand and a small
bunch of flowers in the other.)*

TITANIA	Are you Mr Mifflin? I'm Titania Chapman.
AUBREY	*(obviously impressed)* I say!
ROGER	Yes, yes, my dear. I am Roger Miflin, proprietor of this establishment. Let me take your suitcase and…and…things…
AUBREY	*(pushing in and taking the suitcase)* No, let me. Aubrey Gilbert is my name. I have had the honour to do some work for your father's advertising account.
TITANIA	*(extending her hand)* Oh yes! Mother told me about you. She said you were going to introduce me to the social life of ordinary people…is that right?
AUBREY	*(shaking her hand and not letting it go)* I shall certainly take pleasure in introducing you to some social life – if that is convenient?
TITANIA	*(enthusiastically)* Oh yes! I'm determined to experience, to the full, the life of an ordinary working girl. You may let go of my hand now, Mr Gilbert.
AUBREY	*(hastily letting go)* Oh, sorry!
TITANIA	*(to ROGER)* I bought these flowers for your wife.
ROGER	*(taking them and laying them on the desk)* How kind, Miss Chapman!
TITANIA	Not at all. Mummy has told me so much about you. She

wants me to learn everything I possibly can and I'm determined to show her that I can do it. You mustn't believe a word of what Mummy says, you know. Just because she never sees me reading doesn't mean I'm not crazy about books. By the way...is this bookshop really haunted?

ROGER   Well, until yesterday, I would have said no...but I am beginning to believe that we may have a poltergeist.

TITANIA   Really? What fun!

ROGER   Well, it's actually very irritating. A book disappeared, then reappeared and now it's disappeared again.

AUBREY   Not Carlyle's Cromwell again?

ROGER   The very same. After Mrs Steiner was taken away last night, I went to get the book, which was here on my desk and the blessed thing had gone again.

AUBREY   Extraordinary. That book does seem to have a life of its own.

TITANIA   Oh! You mentioned Mrs Steiner. *(To AUBREY)* I wonder if I might have my suitcase back, Mr Gilbert, only I have a letter in it that Mummy said must be delivered to Mr Mifflin.

    (AUBREY gives TITANIA her suitcase back. She puts it on the desk, opens it and takes out an envelope, which she hands to ROGER. He opens it and reads.)

ROGER   *(reading out loud)* "Dear Mr and Mrs Mifflin, This letter is to let you know that I am leaving your employ immediately. I have secured a job onboard the Isle de France and shall be starting there next week. Also, I am expecting an important package to be delivered to your shop tomorrow, so could my husband call and collect it and any wages that I am owed, please? I was intending to give a week's notice but, obviously, I am in hospital and will not be able to work the week. Yours sincerely, Gladys Steiner." Oh dear, I feel the wrath of Mrs Mifflin brewing as we speak.

AUBREY   *(thoughtful)* Isle de France, eh? I seem to be hearing a great deal about that ship, recently...

ROGER   I can't imagine why a woman of Mrs Steiner's age should decide to go to sea!

AUBREY   No, quite.

ROGER   *(To TITANIA)* Tell me, my dear. Do we have a progress report on Mrs Steiner's health from your mother?

TITANIA   Oh, yes. She said that it was a sprained ankle, nothing more serious. The hospital feels that with bed rest and ice packs she will be as good as new in a few days.

ROGER   Oh well that's a relief! At least she won't be suing us for a broken ankle and loss of earnings.

(HELEN appears.)

HELEN   *(advancing and holding out her hand)* Ah! You must be Miss Titania Chapman! I'm so pleased to meet you!

TITANIA   *(shaking her hand)* Likewise Mrs Mifflin. I think it's adorable of you to take me in. You must let me earn my keep. I mean to dust and wash up and all that sort of thing.

HELEN   Please call me Helen. And I hope that household chores won't be necessary once we get Mrs Steiner back...

ROGER   *(hastily)* Yes, about that, my dear...

HELEN   *(sighing)* What now, Roger?

ROGER	There's a letter.... *(he hands it to HELEN who swiftly reads it)*
HELEN	Well, really! It looks like you may have to help with the washing up after all, Titania!
ROGER	Sorry.
HELEN	Well, for once, I don't think this is your fault, dear. The woman has obviously found a better paid job and was leaving anyway. I just hope the passengers on the Isle de France know what they're letting themselves in for. Anyway, let me take you upstairs, Titania, and show you your room... Mr Gilbert...
AUBREY	Aubrey, please.
HELEN	Aubrey. Would you be a dear and help us up the stairs with our luggage? My suitcase is in the parlour.
AUBREY	Happy to.
	(HELEN leads the way into the parlour. TITANIA and AUBREY follow. AUBREY has already picked up TITANIA's suitcase from the desk.)
HELEN	This is our downstairs parlour which we really only use when the shop is still open and we need to be nearby. Everything else happens upstairs. I'll lead the way
	(HELEN and TITANIA exit "upstairs". AUBREY picks up HELEN's suitcase in his other hand and follows. Just then, ROGER spots MR WEINTRAUB (who is unseen to the audience) passing in the street outside. He rushes to the door and opens it.)
ROGER	*(calling)* Mr Weintraub! Mr Weintraub! *(he rushes out)*

(AUBREY comes back. Speaking as he goes into the shop.)

AUBREY   She's an awfully nice girl, Mifflin....oh! *(realising no-one is there, he looks behind the book stacks and under the desk)* Don't tell me you've disappeared now!

(ROGER comes back into the shop, slightly breathless.)

Oh there you are! I thought you'd disappeared, like the book!

ROGER   What? Oh no. I just saw Weintraub passing by. I thought I'd catch him and tell him that I had the book but I'd lost it again. He said he didn't need it now, anyway. Strange man.

(HELEN and TITANIA reappear and come into the shop. TITANIA is clutching a notepad and pencil.)

TITANIA   ...no, really, I think it's perfectly lovely. And the bed seems so comfortable.

HELEN   Well, that's a relief.

ROGER   Helen, my dear, Titania bought you a bunch of flowers. They're here. *(He hands them to HELEN)*

HELEN   Oh, how thoughtful! You are a kind girl. Now, I shall go and put these in water and make a start on tonight's dinner. And I shall leave you, Titania, to learn all about the trade of bookselling from my strange husband! Mr Gilbert... Aubrey...I shall expect you to come to dinner as well.

AUBREY   Well thank you very much, Mrs Mifflin. I shall be delighted.

HELEN   *(with a look at TITANIA and a smile)* Yes, I thought you might. *(HELEN exits "upstairs.")*

AUBREY   If you'll excuse me, Miss Chapman, I really must go and call on one of my customers before dinnertime. What time shall I return, Mifflin?

ROGER   Oh, about seven o'clock will be fine.

AUBREY   See you later then. *(AUBREY exits through the front door, whistling to himself.)*

TITANIA   Mr Gilbert seems like a very nice man.

ROGER   He is. He's a capital fellow. And since he read Ivanhoe he's been positively transformed.

TITANIA   Really? Books can do that to people then?

ROGER   Oh they can change a person's life! Absolutely!

TITANIA   Well, I'm all ready, Mr Mifflin. I've brought a nice sharp pencil with me to make out sales slips and I've been practising sticking it in my hair. *(She sticks the pencil through her hair and behind her ear.)* I hope you have some of those big red books with all the carbon paper in and everything. I've been watching the girls at Fortnum and Masons make them out and I think they're fascinating. And you must teach me to run the lifts. I'm awfully keen on lifts.

ROGER   Bless me! I'm afraid you'll find us very different from Fortnum and Masons. We haven't any lifts or sales slips, or even a cash register. We don't wait on customers unless they ask us to. They come in and browse around, and if they find anything they want, they come to my desk and ask about it. The cashbox is here and I enter each sale in a little ledger. When you sell a book, you write it down here and the price paid for it.

TITANIA   But suppose it's charged?

ROGER   No charge accounts. Everything is cash. If someone comes in to sell books, you must refer him to me. You mustn't be surprised to see people drop in here and spend several hours reading. Lots of them look on this place as a kind of club.

TITANIA   I understand. I would love to see the worms!

ROGER   Worms?

TITANIA   Bookworms. Mummy says you have lots of them.

ROGER   *(chuckling)* Oh bookworms! Well, you'll see lots of them, alright. They come in and out. Tomorrow I'll show you how my stock is arranged. It'll take you quite a while to get familiar with it. Until then I just want you to poke around and see what there is, until you know the shelves so well you could put your hand on any given book in the dark. That's a game my wife and I used to play. We would turn off all the lights at night and I would call out the name of a book and see how near she could come to finding it. Then I would take a turn. If we couldn't get to within six inches of the book we would pay a forfeit. Great fun!

TITANIA   What larks we'll have! I do think this is a jolly place!

ROGER   *(taking her behind the desk)* And this is the bulletin board, where I put up notices about books that interest me and other stuff I need. Here's a card, I've just been writing. *(He picks up a large piece of card from the desk)*. I'll read it to you. "The Book That Could Have Prevented The War. Now that the fighting is over is a good time to read Thomas Hardy's The Dynasts. I don't want to sell it, because it is one of the greatest treasures I own. But if anyone will guarantee to read all three volumes, and let them sink into his mind, I'm willing to lend them. If enough thoughtful Germans had read The Dynasts before July, 1914, there would have been no war. If every delegate to the forthcoming Peace

Conference could be made to read it before the sessions begin, there would be no more wars." *(ROGER pins the card up on the board.)*

TITANIA   Dear me! Is it as good as all that? Perhaps I'd better read it.

ROGER   It is so good that if I knew any way of doing so, I'd insist on the Prime Minister reading it on his way to France. I wish I could get it on to the ship. My what a book! It makes one positively ill with pity and terror. Sometimes I wake up at night and imagine I can hear Thomas Hardy laughing. But he's a bit too hard for you to tackle.

(HELEN comes back into the shop)

HELEN   Well, dinner won't be long now. I do hope, Titania, that Roger hasn't been terrifying you with all his strange nonsense about books.

TITANIA   No, no. I find it quite fascinating. Mr Mifflin is so incredibly knowledgeable.

HELEN   Mm. He's that alright. But his obsessions with books do tend to make him a little carried away with things. We had a dog once. Lovely old thing who sadly died but Roger insisted on building him a kennel that was a replica of the British Library Reading Room, with imitation book shelves along the outside.

TITANIA   How ingenious!

HELEN   Yes it was. He spent weeks thinking of books that he could translate into dog titles, like The Rubaiyat of Omar Canine; The works of Bone-ar Law and so on.

TITANIA   Amazing!

HELEN   Where's Aubrey?

ROGER	He had a few business calls to make before dinner. He'll be back soon.
HELEN	I think I rather approve of that young man. He seems rather dashing. Is he, Roger?
ROGER	Oh, very. A former intelligence officer in the Army. I suspect he may have done some very brave things but he's too modest to go into detail.
TITANIA	He's very nice-looking…I mean…I would imagine that some girls might think that…
HELEN	*(smiling)* Mm. I imagine some girls might indeed. Come along, Titania. I'm sure you've had enough bookselling for today. You have to take it in small doses, you know, otherwise it gives you a headache.
TITANIA	*(writing it on her pad)* Headache. I can see that the business of bookselling is far more dangerous than people give it credit for. What with Thomas Hardy making one ill and the danger of headaches. Why, it's more hazardous than the munitions industry!
HELEN	Oh dear. I can see Roger's been filling your head with all sorts of nonsense. Come along dear. I think a large sherry before dinner might perk you up.
	(HELEN shepherds TITANIA "upstairs.")
ROGER	*(calling)* I won't be long! I'm just going to have another look for that Cromwell book. *(He starts to sift through all the books and papers on his desk when the phone rings.)* Hallo?…yes, this is Roger Mifflin….yes, as a matter of fact I do buy books…in order to give them a decent home you understand…oh you do? …a large quantity?…well, I would

have to have a look at them…Tunbridge Wells?...dear me, that is a bit of a journey…yes, I'm sure it will be worth it… yes, of course, Mr…? Mitchell…let me write the address down…*(he grabs a notepad and pencil)* The Cedars, Mountfield Road, Tunbridge Wells…not far from the station…good. Eleven o'clock? Yes, I should be able to manage that…good day, Mr Mitchell. *(He puts the phone down).*

(AUBREY enters the shop)

Ah, my dear chap, I wonder if I could ask you a favour?

AUBREY   Ask away.

ROGER   I've just had a phone call from a gentleman in Tunbridge Wells who has a large collection of books to sell. It's too good an opportunity to pass up – even though it is rather a journey. I shall have to get up at the crack of dawn. I just wondered if you could pop into the shop now and then to make sure that my wife and Miss Chapman are managing. Would you be able to do that for me?

AUBREY   It would be a pleasure. I'm working around this area tomorrow anyway. I'll pop in every hour or so. Would that do?

ROGER   Absolutely splendid! Now come along and have some dinner. If my sense of smell is not being deceived, I think my wife has some of her wonderful beef stew simmering. I'll just lock up and we will eat.

AUBREY   Capital.

(ROGER goes to the shop door and turns the key in the lock, then he turns the sign over and puts the key on the desk.)

ROGER   I was looking for that Cromwell book when the phone rang. It's definitely not on my desk anywhere. I do wonder what happened to it.

AUBREY   Do you know…I've been thinking about that. I reckon the Steiner woman took it. She was the last person at your desk after you had put the book there.

ROGER   Gracious me! Whatever would she want such a book for? First Mr Weintraub and now Mrs Steiner. Perhaps there has been some recommendation in the German press about the book. I suppose that's possible.

AUBREY   It's been gnawing away at me and I don't suppose I shall get any peace until I've figured it out.

HELEN   *(offstage)* Roger! Dinner is about to be served!

ROGER   *(calling)* Righto! Food, at last. Come along Aubrey. Thoughts about Carlyle's Cromwell must be pushed aside by beef.

           (ROGER and AUBREY exit "upstairs".)

MUSIC.

FADE TO BLACK.

END OF ACT 1.

THE HAUNTED BOOKSHOP

ACT II

SCENE 1

*The next day in the book shop. It is early evening. (TITANIA is sitting at
the desk writing in the ledger. HELEN is packing a cardboard box with
several books.)*

HELEN	Trust Roger to be absent on the busiest day of the year!
TITANIA	Yes, it's been frantic, hasn't it? I hope I've acquitted myself well. I'm sure I hadn't a clue what I was doing most of the time but there just wasn't time to think!
HELEN	You did wonderfully, dear. Apart from the little mix-up when the man asked for a book about Grace Darling and you took him to the bird section.
TITANIA	Oh, yes! I'm awfully sorry about that but he did mumble so and I thought he wanted a book about the "grey starling".
HELEN	Perfectly understandable. I did laugh at the look on his face though!
TITANIA	We do seem to have sold an awful lot of war poetry today.
HELEN	*(sighing)* Yes. You really would think that people would want to put all that behind them now we have put an end to the madness. Just now, in the intoxication of the German collapse, everyone is rejoicing in a new happiness. But the real peace will be a long time coming. When you tear up all the fibres of civilisation it's a slow job to knit things together again. When they are taught in schools that war is the most

loathsome scourge of humanity, then there may be some
hope for the future. But I'd like to bet that they are having it
drilled into them that war is a glorious and noble sacrifice.
The people who write about the divine frenzy of battle are
usually those who dipped their pens a long, long way from
the hell of the trenches. Except for Seigfried Sasson, I think.
Have you read his poems?

TITANIA   No.

HELEN   You should. They're brutal. And very effective. Personally, I
think any man would be a traitor to humanity if he didn't
spend every effort of his waking life to try and make war
impossible in the future.

TITANIA   True. But I'm afraid I do think the war was very glorious as
well as very terrible. Lots of chaps that I know went over,
knowing full well what they were going to face and yet went
gladly and humbly in the thought that they were going for a
true cause.

HELEN   Mm. A cause which is so true shouldn't need the sacrifice of
millions of fine lives. Don't imagine that I don't see the
dreadful nobility of it. But don't you suppose that the
Germans thought that they too were marching off for a
noble cause – even though they began it and forced this
dreadful misery on the world? They had been educated to
believe so, for at least a generation. That's the terrible
hypnotism of war – the brute mass impulse, the pride and
national spirit, the instinctive simplicity of men that makes
them worship what is their own above everything else.
Music and flags and men marching in step have bewitched
me, like everyone else, but then I have gone home and

thanked God that I didn't have a son to send to war and that my husband was too old.

TITANIA   People can't help loving their country, though, can they?

HELEN   Of course not. I love my country so much that I want to see her take the lead in making a new era possible. We had to beat Germany, of course, but the absurdity lies in the fact that we have beaten ourselves in doing it. The first thing you'll find is that when this Peace Conference starts, we'll have to help Germany on to her feet again so that she can be punished in an orderly way. We shall have to feed her and admit her back into the world so that she can pay her way and we shall have to police her cities to make sure that the German people don't riot or go mad. The upshot of it all is that the men who fought the most terrible war in history – our men – will have done it for the privilege of nursing their enemy back to health. If that isn't an absurdity, I don't know what is? That's what happens when a great nation like Germany goes insane. Goodness! I have become serious! I'm so sorry dear! I don't usually drone on like this about politics. That's usually Roger's province.

TITANIA   No. Don't apologise. I've learnt something from you. People think my generation is awfully feckless, I know they do – because we behave like foolish children half the time. But I think it's because those men who are left are giddy with relief that it's all over and the women are just hysterical at the thought of the future. Lots of them thought they would just get married and have children – I suppose I did. But that's not going to happen now.

(AUBREY enters the shop, cheerfully)

HELEN	*(Almost to herself)* I wouldn't be so sure about that. *(raising her voice in mock exasperation)* Aubrey! This is the tenth time you have visited us today? Did Roger put you up to this?
AUBREY	*(sheepishly)* Well, I suppose he did. He just asked me to pop in now and then and make sure you were both alright.
HELEN	I've been running this bookshop ever since I married Roger. He should know by now that I can cope! However, I appreciate the thought and I shall give him a big hug when he returns. Do you think you could be of invaluable service, Aubrey, and hold the flaps of this box down whilst I tie it with string?
AUBREY	I'm your man.
	(AUBREY holds the top of the cardboard box down, whilst HELEN ties it around with string. They continue talking.)
	It seems to have been jolly busy today.
HELEN	It certainly does. I do believe that the general populace got wind of Roger being away and decided to rush in and simply buy a book, without the inconvenience of a lecture from Roger on the value of literature.
AUBREY	*(laughing)* You may be right! How are you getting on, Miss Chapman?
TITANIA	Oh I've had a marvellous day! It's quite exciting earning a living. I could get quite used to it. In fact, once or twice today, I experienced a feeling of elation that I've never quite experienced before. Actually selling things makes me feel quite giddy!
HELEN	*(looking at AUBREY)* There's no hope for the girl! I think Roger's insanity may be catching.

(The telephone rings. TITANIA picks it up.)

TITANIA   The Haunted Book Shop...Miss Chapman speaking.

(HELEN looks at AUBREY and raises her eyebrows at TITANIA's professionalism.)

Oh, hallo Mr Mifflin! We've had the most marvellous day!...Yes lots of customers...I'll pass you over to her...*(To HELEN)* It's Mr Mifflin.

HELEN   We'll have to swap places. You carry on tying this parcel and I'll sit down.

(They swap places. AUBREY stares intently at TITANIA, who is now very close to him. She occasionally looks at him and smiles.)

Roger? Where are you? I expected you to be on your way home by now?...Oh really?...how odd!...You poor thing!...no, no...of course you can't...Aubrey? Yes, he's here... *(To AUBREY)* Roger wants to speak to you. You'll have to come over here, the phone won't stretch that far.

(AUBREY and HELEN swap places. AUBREY has to squeeze past TITANIA and he seems to be getting a bit hot under the collar.)

AUBREY   Yes, old man...I say, that is odd!...very suspicious, I agree...I do, yes, in my room...no problem...absolutely, old man...think nothing of it...*(to HELEN)* He wants to speak to you again.

HELEN   Right.

(They swap places again but this time AUBREY goes around the front of the desk.)

What is it dear?...oh nonsense! That's not necessary at all!...no, alright...I understand...if that's what you wish, I'll abide by it, but I really think you are over-reacting...no, no, alright...I said I would abide by your wishes...now take care dear...find yourself a nice little hotel and stop worrying. We'll be fine...yes, yes...I will. Goodbye dear. *(She replaces the mouthpiece.)* Well! This is a pretty kettle of fish!

TITANIA   What's happened?

HELEN   Roger has been led a merry dance in Tunbridge Wells, looking for an address that doesn't exist. He finally went to the police station and they told him that no such address is listed in Tunbridge Wells – by which time he had missed the last train back to London. He's awfully cross about being duped by some prankster and he's rather worried about our safety. Which is why – even though I told him he was foolish – he wants Aubrey to stay the night and protect us.

TITANIA   *(wide-eyed)* Oh!

AUBREY   I don't want to alarm you but he also wants me to fetch my old service revolver.

HELEN   Well, really! Whatever has got into Roger?!

AUBREY   Obviously, the whole Tunbridge Wells experience has really unsettled him but I think he's being very sensible.

HELEN   That's all very well, Aubrey, but I have no spare room upstairs in which you can sleep.

AUBREY   Oh, I think I should be downstairs anyway. And I'm perfectly used to sleeping in an armchair. I got used to it during the war, you know.

HELEN   Good grief. This whole day is turning into something quite strange. I've never known Roger be so excitable about my safety before. I've travelled all over the place on my own and he's barely registered that I'm away until it gets to dinner time!

AUBREY   Yes, well, as I said before, I think the whole Tunbridge Wells business has jangled his nerves. Better to be safe than sorry. I'll just go back to my lodgings and fetch the you-know-what. I shan't be a moment. *(AUBREY exits)*

TITANIA   It's awfully thrilling, isn't it?

HELEN   I suppose it is. Worrying too, though. This is most unlike Roger.

TITANIA   I never thought I should be in the situation where I would be staying in this shop under armed guard!

HELEN   Goodness knows what your mother will think!

TITANIA   Oh, I don't think we should tell Mummy. Some things are best kept from parents, you know. Especially when guns are involved.

           (MRS CHAPMAN suddenly appears at the front door and waves before entering.)

HELEN   Oh my God! Your mother is here!

TITANIA   *(whispering)* Not one word, Mrs Mifflin. Just pretend that nothing has happened. *(to MRS C)* Mummy! Are you checking up on me?

MRS C   Goodness, no! I just happened to be passing on my way to that lovely parfumerie at the end of the street. My sister has a birthday soon and I do feel that she would adore some perfume. How are things?

TITANIA	Wonderful! We've had the most frantic day! Haven't we, Mrs Mifflin?
HELEN	You could say that, yes.
TITANIA	The book-buying public has beaten a path to our door and we've sold tons of books.
MRS C	Marvellous! *(to HELEN)* And has my daughter been useful in all this hurly burly of commerce, Mrs Mifflin?
HELEN	She's been excellent. Titania has taken to the book trade like a duck to water! Can I offer you a cup of tea, Mrs Chapman?
MRS C	Do you know, that would be lovely! I've been shopping all afternoon and I'm absolutely parched.
HELEN	Well, I'll just pop up and put the kettle on. Do sit down, I shan't be long.
	(HELEN goes "upstairs" and MRS C sits in the armchair near the front door and takes her gloves off.)
MRS C	I'm so pleased that you are making yourself useful, Titania. Your father will be very happy too. Neither of us hold with young ladies being simply ornaments and lounging about the place. A spell of work will be so good for your soul.
TITANIA	Well, I must admit, Mummy, I was a bit resentful when you both said I should go out to work but I've had such fun here in the last two days! A bookshop is so much more interesting than an ordinary department store. One meets such interesting people.
	(AUBREY enters, not seeing MRS C.)
AUBREY	Right, I've got it…

TITANIA	*(hastily)* Er…Mr Gilbert! How nice of you to drop in! How unexpected! *(she makes signs that her mother is behind him)*
AUBREY	*(looking confused, then turning and seeing MRS C.)* Ah! Mrs Chapman! So good to see you again! *(he shakes her hand)*
MRS C	And I'm very pleased to see you as well, Mr Gilbert. What exactly is it that you have "got"?
AUBREY	Pardon?
MRS C	When you came in you said "Right, I've got it…"
	(There is a pause, whilst AUBREY does some quick thinking.)
AUBREY	Ah…er…*(an idea comes to him)* Book title! Yes, that's it! I've got the name of a book I want to purchase! *(turning to TITANIA)* Ivanhoe! That's it! Ivanhoe!
TITANIA	I shall see if I can find it.
	(TITANIA goes behind the bookshelves and HELEN appears with a tray of tea things and puts them on the desk.)
HELEN	Ah, Aubrey! We haven't seen you for a while – how are things?
AUBREY	*(playing along)* Oh, busy, you know. Very busy.
	(TITANIA re-appears with the book)
TITANIA	There we are Mr.Gilbert. Ivanhoe. That will be sixpence please.
AUBREY	Yes. *(fishing in his pockets)* Sixpence. There you are, Miss Chapman.
	(TITANIA takes the money and puts it in the cash box.)
HELEN	Won't you join us in a cup of tea, Mr Gilbert?

AUBREY	That would be very pleasant, Mrs Mifflin. Thank you.
	(HELEN dispenses tea to everyone, talking as she does so.)
HELEN	Titania and I were discussing politics before you both came in.
	(MRS C nearly chokes on her tea.)
MRS C	Politics? With Titania?
HELEN	Yes. More specifically, we were discussing the war and the upcoming Peace Conference.
MRS C	Ah, yes. My husband's the one who has forthright opinions on the Peace Conference. He believes that all these things should be sorted out by businessmen not politicians or generals. As he frequently says to me, "Who better to sort out feeding the war-ravaged countries of Europe than food manufacturers?" He maintains that they have far more experience of supply and logistics than Lloyd George or General Haig.
AUBREY	I think your husband is right, Mrs Chapman. My personal experience of generals, during the last four years, is that they couldn't organise a chimpanzee's tea party, let alone provisioning most of Europe. And as for the politicians – well, they got us into the whole bally mess in the first place.
HELEN	Quite. Actually, I think that the whole business of peace and its ramifications should be left to women. Look how magnificently the Women's Auxiliaries organised nursing, transport, communications, food supplies, convalescence and God knows what else, during the war! I'm sure they could have everything shipshape in no time.
AUBREY	I would second that. Many of the men who went to war would never have had any letters, food parcels or comforts

of any kind if it weren't for the organisational skills of British women. Mind you, I think even the most fearsome British nanny would be hard-pressed to keep post-war Germany in line. Only the toughest measures are going to stop Germany re-arming and becoming a worldwide threat again. It's going to take all the Allies and their professional armies to keep Germany in its place.

TITANIA   Is that what they're proposing?

AUBREY   What?

TITANIA   To send fresh soldiers over the Germany to act as policemen?

AUBREY   I shouldn't be surprised. The American President has been quite vocal about how Germany should be punished for the devastation it caused in Europe.

MRS C   Yes. Woodrow Wilson's coming over on the Isle de France isn't he? And picking up Lloyd George on the way, I hear. I bet they shall have it all worked out by the time they dock at Le Havre.

AUBREY   (A thought has occurred to him but it isn't quite fully formed so he speaks half to himself) Yes…both of them on the same ship…that's right…

HELEN   Are you alright, Aubrey?

AUBREY   (a bit vague) What? (pulling himself together) Oh, sorry, Mrs Mifflin! I was just thinking about something…sorry.

MRS C   Well, the tea was lovely, Mrs Mifflin and I must be going now. It's getting quite dark and I must catch the parfumerie before it closes. (She gathers up her gloves and bag and goes over to TITANIA to kiss her cheek) Now be a good girl for the Mifflins, my dear. I'm very pleased with the way it's all going, so far.

(MRS C exits)

TITANIA	Well! That was a close shave!
AUBREY	I very nearly gave the whole game away, didn't I?
TITANIA	Very nearly – but you expertly got yourself out of it. Here's your sixpence back, by the way. *(She gives him the money.)* I'll put the book back where it belongs. *(AUBREY gives her the book.)* *(TITANIA goes behind the bookshelves to return the book)*
HELEN	*(whispering to AUBREY)* She's very intelligent, you know.
AUBREY	*(whispering back)* And rather good-looking too.
	(TITANIA returns.)
HELEN	So, I think we should close the shop now and have an early dinner. Then, I shall take my sleeping medication and retire. I suppose I can rely on your honour, Mr Gilbert, to remain downstairs, once I'm asleep?
AUBREY	*(shocked)* Good Lord! You don't think I would…Good Lord!
HELEN	Well, I'm sorry to have embarrassed you, Aubrey, but I do have a young lady in my care and I felt that I had to ask the question.
TITANIA	*(gleefully)* Poor Mr Gilbert has gone quite red!
AUBREY	I can assure you, ladies, on my honour as a gentleman, I shall take up residence in one of the armchairs in the parlour and I shall not move. Unless, of course, it were to rush upstairs to rescue you from a fire or something.
HELEN	You're a good chap. It's just that once I take my sleeping draught I'm dead to the world and I have to know that I am able to trust you.
AUBREY	On my honour, Mrs Mifflin.

HELEN   Good. Lock up the shop, Titania. And let's go upstairs and
                 have a hearty dinner. It's getting very cold at night now. I
                 think I need to draw the fire up a little, don't you?

                 *(HELEN goes "upstairs". TITANIA locks the front door,
                 turns the sign over and puts the key on the table. AUBREY
                 waits for her.)*

AUBREY   Look…Miss Chapman…I'm very sorry if you were
                 embarrassed by Mrs Mifflin's questions. I just want to
                 assure you that I wouldn't dream of coming upstairs during
                 the night. You are perfectly safe with me.

TITANIA   *(playfully)* I'm sure I am, Mr Gilbert. But remember, I didn't
                 promise not to come downstairs, did I?

                 *(She laughs and runs "upstairs", leaving AUBREY rooted to
                 the spot.)*

AUBREY   *(In a horrified whisper)* Good Lord!

MUSIC.

FADE TO BLACK.

END OF SCENE 1.

THE HAUNTED BOOKSHOP

ACT II

SCENE 2.

About midnight. There is no light in the bookshop or parlour, except for moonlight streaming in from the shop front door and the window in the parlour. The curtain between the shop and the parlour has been drawn back and AUBREY is seated in an armchair, which he has turned to face the shop. He has put the table beside him and on it is his revolver. TITANIA enters quietly from "upstairs". She is wearing a nightdress and silk dressing gown. She is carrying a blanket.

TITANIA   *(loud whisper)* Has anything happened yet?

AUBREY   *(also loud whisper)* Good Lord! You made me jump! I could have shot you, you silly girl!

TITANIA   *(speaking quietly but not whispering)* Sorry. I just thought you might need a blanket.

AUBREY   *(also speaking quietly but not whispering)* I don't intend sleeping, Miss Chapman. The purpose of my being here is to guard you both.

TITANIA   Well, still, it's quite cold. You might need the extra covering.

AUBREY   *(getting up and taking the blanket)* Thank you. Now please go back to bed before you catch your death. Especially wandering around dressed like that. *(He goes back and sits down in his chair.)*

TITANIA   *(a little irritated)* I do wish you would stop treating me as though I am a child.

AUBREY   *(feeling a bit awkward)* Look, Miss Chapman. I know that
           you are an emancipated woman but I think that coming
           downstairs in your nightclothes is a little too emancipated
           for me to cope with.

TITANIA   I haven't come down here to seduce you – so you needn't
           worry about that!

AUBREY   *(exasperated)* Well, really! You seem determined to
           embarrass me!

TITANIA   Oh do stop it, Aubrey! The world has changed since the war.
           Men and women are on an equal footing now, after all
           we've been through. I think false modesty and Victorian
           behaviour is out of place in society now.

           *(TITANIA flounces across the room and sits in the other
           armchair, sulking. An exasperated AUBREY turns his chair
           around slightly so that he can see TITANIA but still look at
           the shop.)*

AUBREY   The trouble with young women is that they fail to grasp that
           men fought the war so that things in England could stay the
           same. Do you honestly think that you would have got men
           to go willingly into that awful carnage if they did not feel
           that they were doing it to protect their women and children
           back home?

TITANIA   No, I suppose not.

AUBREY   Then, when we do come home, the blasted goalposts have
           been moved! It's not a wonder a lot of men are bitter.

TITANIA   I don't understand you.

AUBREY   Look. We were all told that we would be returning to "a
           land fit for heroes" – and what did we find? Most of the

manufacturing jobs have been taken by women, and the employers actually prefer them, and so the men can't get their jobs back. One of my sergeants used to work on an assembly line in a factory making nuts and bolts. When he comes back, he's told that the women are quicker at the job; they have nimbler fingers; they concentrate better; production has improved and so he couldn't get his job back. I was an actuary an insurance company before I got called up and when I got back they'd replaced me with a woman and were reluctant to give her the sack because she was the sole breadwinner of her family, her husband having been killed at the Somme. Now I don't begrudge that lady my job. She has mouths to feed and I was lucky that I got another job through a captain in my regiment. But a lot of men weren't so lucky. The women that they fought to protect are no longer in need of protection and they are confused. We're all confused. Respectable women are shortening their hemlines, smoking cigarettes, drinking in public houses without male escorts – it takes a lot of getting used to. And you – coming downstairs in the middle of the night in your dressing gown – well – it's something that a respectable woman would *never* have done four years ago and I'm sorry if that makes me sound old-fashioned.

TITANIA   *(smiling)* I think it's sweet that you're old fashioned. In fact, I rather like it that you're so chivalrous.

AUBREY   *(irritated)* You make me sound like an old fogey. Mifflin was right, you know, when he gave me Ivanhoe to read. He knew that what I needed was a good dose of old-fashioned heroism and chivalry. Reading about a knight rescuing damsels in distress was just the pick-me-up I needed. The book should be given to all returning soldiers – except that, I suppose, it might make them even more depressed.

TITANIA   The thing is, though, not all men are like you – and my father, of course. Not all men look after their women – cherish them and protect them. If you read some of the Suffragette pamphlets you would realise that lots of women – not just working class women either – are married to men who beat them or treat them like slaves.

AUBREY   Yes, well, I don't know any man like that – nor would I care to. Look here! Have you just come downstairs to annoy me?

TITANIA   No, I actually came downstairs to get to know you better – and I think I have.

AUBREY   What does that mean?

TITANIA   Well, I don't have a great experience of men…

AUBREY   *(interrupting)* I should hope not! How old are you?

TITANIA   Isn't that a rather impertinent question?

AUBREY   *(smiling)* Hah! You can't fall back on Victorian values just when it suits you. You're an emancipated woman so therefore I can feel free to ask you your age.

TITANIA   If you must know I'm twenty six – which four years ago would have made me a shameful spinster. Under the old values, I should have been married by the time I was twenty. Twenty two at the very latest. Fortunately times have changed. As I was saying, before you interrupted me, I don't have a great experience of men but I was curious that you seemed too good to be true.

AUBREY   *(confused)* Too good to be true? Is that an insult?

TITANIA   Not at all! What I meant was that here I was, introduced to a good looking man in his thirties, seemingly decent, hard-working, obliging and chivalrous. I mean you might have walked out of the pages of a penny romance! I didn't think men like you existed any more, except in fiction.

AUBREY   *(not quite sure what to make of her statement)* Hm. Well, if you say so, but I know plenty of decent chaps. Maybe you just don't mix in the right circles.

TITANIA   I think you may be right. You see the problem with coming from a family with lots of money is that one tends to mix with the upper classes a lot – even though one is – as I was constantly reminded – coming from a *trade* background. Most of the young men I met, before the war, were titled or well connected and, I'm sorry to say, complete idiots. The trouble is that when one's father is a self-made man, one has certain standards of behaviour. Most of the men I used to meet wouldn't have known what a work ethic was if it fell on their heads. You know, despite my mother's conviction that I am a complete flibberty gibbet, I am actually quite discerning and I know that I could never marry a man just for his money or title.

AUBREY   *(grudgingly)* Hm. Well perhaps I might revise my opinion of you, then.

TITANIA   *(mocking)* How kind of you.

AUBREY   But, look, I promised Mrs Mifflin that I wouldn't take advantage of the situation and you, coming downstairs, has put me in an awkward position. I'm perfectly happy to talk to you and tell you my whole life story but I would rather do it over lunch in a nice restaurant. Dinner even. How about it?

TITANIA	Are you asking me out?
AUBREY	Yes. That's the gist of it.
TITANIA	I accept. Dinner on Friday night. And you can take me to see the new Tarzan film at the picture house as well.
AUBREY	Fine. As long as you go back to bed. Otherwise the deal's off.
TITANIA	Fine. I shall go back to bed then. *(TITANIA gets up and goes over to him.)* You're really quite forceful, aren't you?
AUBREY	Bed, now.

(TITANIA quickly bends down and gives him a kiss on the cheek, then scuttles back "upstairs". AUBREY is taken aback, but then he grins.)

(to himself) Hussy!

(AUBREY re-positions his chair so that he is facing the shop again. Suddenly, we see a man's shape outside the shop door. AUBREY picks up his revolver very slowly. The man outside the door takes a key from his pocket and unlocks the door quietly, then he opens it an inch and reaches his hand up to take hold of the bell and prevent it from ringing when he opens the door further. As he comes into the shop we see that he is wearing a balaclava and his face cannot be seen. He fiddles about at the front bookshelves, making some space, then he takes a book from his pocket and places it amongst the other books. AUBREY stands up very slowly, while this is going on and then steps through the opening into the shop.)

AUBREY	*(loudly)* Stop where you are! I have a gun!

(The man panics and makes for the door. AUBREY fires a shot and misses. There is a scream from upstairs. The man

bolts into the street and AUBREY runs after him. TITANIA
appears in the doorway to "upstairs" with her hand clasped
to her mouth in fear. An altercation is heard offstage, in the
"street".)

AUBREY   *(offstage)* Come back here you....now I've got you....Aagh!

              (AUBREY comes staggering back into the shop and
              collapses on the floor. TITANIA rushes to the opening and
              seeing AUBREY hurt, rushes over to him.)

TITANIA   Aubrey! Aubrey! Speak to me!

AUBREY   *(rolling over on his back and moaning)* Ooh! Damn fellow
              coshed me on the head with something. Lock the door,
              quickly!

              (TITANIA runs and gets the key, locks the door, and turns
              on the lights. AUBREY sits up, his head in his hands and
              realises there is blood on the back of his head.)

TITANIA   Oh my God! You're bleeding!

AUBREY   Yes. He whacked me pretty hard.

TITANIA   You should go to hospital!

AUBREY   God no! I've cracked my head worse than this playing
              rugby. Are you any good at first aid?

TITANIA   I did go on a course, actually. Mrs Mifflin keeps a first aid
              box in the desk. Let me get it.

              (TITANIA goes to the desk and gets a box out of the
              drawer. She takes out of the box some cotton wool, a bottle
              of iodine and some bandages. Then she comes back to
              AUBREY, kneels behind him and puts some iodine on the
              cotton wool.)

	I'm afraid this is going to hurt rather a lot.
AUBREY	Don't worry, I'll cope.
	(She dabs the iodine-soaked cotton wool on the wound AUBREY arches his back and opens his mouth in a silent scream.)
TITANIA	Sorry, sorry. It's rather deep. I do think you ought to go somewhere and have some stitches.
AUBREY	*(managing to speak)* Well, you may be right, but let's see how I am in the morning, shall we?
	(TITANIA starts to bandage his head, which she does quite expertly. They talk as he does so.)
TITANIA	Who do you think the man was? And why was he here?
AUBREY	I don't know. I have a few ideas but I need to speak to Mifflin first. I suppose one possibility is that he came to kidnap *you*.
TITANIA	Me! Why on earth would anyone want to kidnap me?
AUBREY	Well, I imagine that the daughter of the man who owns ChapmansDaintybits is worth quite a bit of money. You remember me talking about the desperate men, returning from the war, who have no job to come back to? Well, perhaps he thought it would be some easy money to get Mifflin out of the way, kidnap the heiress under his roof and demand a huge ransom. That could be the reason why the man broke in tonight – except I don't think so. For one, he didn't break in – he had a key – and, two, he was fiddling about at the bookshelves. Why would he bother with that, if his sole intent was to kidnap you? Surely he would have gone straight upstairs and done the deed? I don't know. There's more to this than meets the eye but I can't think at

the moment, my head is throbbing so.

TITANIA   Poor Aubrey! There's some aspirin in the first aid box. I think
            you should take two of those and come and lay down on my bed.

AUBREY   God God! You're at it again! Are you determined to
            compromise me, woman?

TITANIA   Don't be ridiculous! *(impishly)* I wouldn't dream of seducing
            a wounded man! What do you take me for? No, you need to
            lie down. You can't sit up in a chair all night – not after a
            blow to the head – and it would be even more compromising
            if I were to help you over the road and into your lodgings. I
            couldn't possibly sleep now, anyway. As soon as you lay
            down, I shall come back down here, with a cup of tea and
            read a magazine or something. You can leave me your
            revolver. I'm a crack shot, you know.

AUBREY   I certainly shan't leave you my revolver! You might shoot
            Mifflin as he comes back in the shop! Or an innocent
            customer! You'll have to read a magazine unarmed. Could
            you possibly help me up?

TITANIA   Of course. *(she helps him to his feet, then puts his arm
            round her shoulder.)* Take it steady now.

            *(They move very slowly towards the parlour. AUBREY
            suddenly stops.)*

AUBREY   I say, have you noticed that Mrs Mifflin hasn't even stirred?

TITANIA   So she hasn't! Well she did say that she sleeps like the dead
            after her sleep medication.

AUBREY   Yes, but even so. All the shouting in the street outside her
            window…

TITANIA   Not to mention the gunshot…which nearly gave me a heart
            attack!

AUBREY   And not so much as a murmur from Mrs M. We'd better
            check that she's alright on our way up.

TITANIA   Yes, I'll pop in her room and give her a prod or two.

AUBREY   You know, if that bounder who bashed me on the head, was
            going to kidnap you – he didn't do his research very well,
            did he?

TITANIA   What do you mean?

AUBREY   Well I would imagine that anyone who knows you could
            have told him that you would be a most difficult person to
            abduct. Argumentative, bold, resourceful and a crackshot.
            That would put me off any kidnap plot straight away!

TITANIA   Are you being insulting?

AUBREY   No, actually, I think I was trying to pay you a compliment. I
            think you're rather admirable.

TITANIA   Thank you. If you weren't so wounded, I would kiss you.

AUBREY   I'm not that wounded…

            *(TITANIA turns to face him and smiles. They very gently
            kiss as the lights fade to black and the music comes up.)*

END OF SCENE 2.

THE HAUNTED BOOKSHOP
ACT II
SCENE 3.

*The next morning. The lights go up to reveal HELEN, AUBREY and
TITANIA all seated around the desk in the bookshop looking decidedly
under the weather. AUBREY still has his head bandaged, and a headache;
HELEN looks rather groggy and has a headache; and TITANIA is suffering
from lack of sleep. There is a tray with tea things on the desk and they all
have cups of tea in front of them. On the armchair by the front door is a pile
of parcels and letters. The first aid box is still out on the desk.*

HELEN	*(opening the first aid box and taking out a bottle of aspirin)* Aspirin anyone?
AUBREY	Yes please.
TITANIA	Mm. Me too.
	(HELEN doles out the aspirin and they all take them.)
HELEN	I don't think I have ever felt this bad after taking that sleeping medicine. I shall have stern words with Mr Weintraub about it. I think he must have made it far too strong.
AUBREY	Does Weintraub always make up your medicine?
HELEN	Yes. And he knows I only take it now and then. I was only joking about it the other day, when I ordered it from him. I told him that the ridiculous thing is that I only take the medicine when Roger is away because I've got so used to the sound of his snoring that I can't get to sleep when everything

is quiet. A bottle usually lasts me for ages because Roger is rarely away for the night. He frets about his books, you understand. Not me – the books.

AUBREY	So Weintraub knew that the medicine would only be used when Mr Mifflin was away?
HELEN	Well, yes. I distinctly remember telling him.
AUBREY	Interesting.
TITANIA	Does that mean anything?
AUBREY	It might.

(ROGER enters the shop, shouting out as he comes in. He is wearing a coat and hat and carrying a briefcase.)

ROGER	I'm back!

(The others all wince and clutch their heads.)

HELEN	Roger! Must you be so loud?
ROGER	Oh dear! Oh dear, dear, dear! Whatever happened in my absence? Aubrey! My dear chap! Your head is bandaged!
AUBREY	Yes, I got hit on the head by an intruder.
ROGER	Oh, my lord! Don't tell me things are so bad that people are breaking in now to steal books!
HELEN	Roger, you're incorrigible! Why must everything always come down to books?
ROGER	Because it always does, my dear. It always does. Is there any tea left in that pot?
HELEN	Help yourself. Have my cup. I've barely touched it.
ROGER	And why are you two ladies looking so wan?
TITANIA	Mrs Mifflin thinks that Mr Weintraub made her sleeping

medicine too strong and I've been up all night, in case the intruder came back.

ROGER Oh this is worse than I thought! Tell me the whole story from beginning to end. *(he draws up a chair and begins to sip his tea.)*

AUBREY I stayed up last night, in a chair in the parlour. Some blaggard let himself in with a key, about midnight. I challenged him and he ran off. I ran after him and he biffed me one on the head with some cosh. I staggered back into the shop, Miss Chapman patched me up and then...

TITANIA *(taking over)* I put him on my bed as he was very groggy and came back down here to stay on guard in case the intruder came back.

HELEN And I slept though it all – fighting, gunshots, everything. I woke up this morning with the mother of all headaches to find a fully-dressed Aubrey spark out on Titania's bed and Titania, poor girl, asleep in a chair in the parlour, clutching your old cricket bat.

ROGER My cricket bat?

TITANIA I was going to biff him over the head with it, if he came back.

AUBREY *(smiling)* Were you really?

TITANIA Of course! Pay him back for what he did to you.

AUBREY I bet you would have done, too.

ROGER But what do we think was the purpose of this nocturnal visit?

TITANIA Aubrey thought it might be to kidnap me and hold me to ransom.

HELEN	Good God! Your mother never would have forgiven me!
AUBREY	Except, in the cold light of day, I have revised my opinion of that theory.
ROGER	Indeed! So what do you think was the purpose now?
AUBREY	*(getting up and pacing around)* I'm not sure. But I don't think it was a simple kidnap plot. I think we are dealing with something altogether different. The way I reason it is this…you get a hoax phone call to get you out of the way… Mrs M is given extra strength sleeping medicine which completely knocks her out…
HELEN	Completely.
AUBREY	A chap comes in here…letting himself in with a key, mind you…
ROGER	Ah! That's interesting!
AUBREY	Quite…and whoever set this little ruse up had no way of knowing that Miss Chapman was here or that I would be here. They expected to do whatever they were going to do and be uninterrupted because Mrs M was flat out upstairs.
ROGER	But what was this intruder going to do?
AUBREY	Beats me. But he was fiddling about with this book case here *(he points to the one by the door)* before I challenged him.
ROGER	Aha! I told you it always comes down to books, didn't I? *(ROGER goes over to the book case and peers at the shelves, then he suddenly pounces on one particular book.)* Bless my soul! It's the Cromwell book again! *(He looks at it, turns it over in his hands and then opens it.)* And that's odd.
AUBREY	What?

ROGER	*(astonished)* It's been re-covered!
HELEN	Oh, don't be so silly, Roger! Are you suggesting that someone came into this book shop, at night, to slyly return a book that he had damaged and had re-covered? Why on earth would anyone do that?
ROGER	I have no idea but this is definitely not the original binding.
AUBREY	Are you sure? It looks the same.
ROGER	The binding has been cleverly imitated but it can't fool me. In the first place, there was rubbed corner at the top and there was an ink stain on one of the end papers. I've had this book long enough to know it by heart. Now what the deuce would anyone want to have it rebound for? And why did it disappear in the first place?
AUBREY	*(having an idea)* Mrs Steiner. It has to be something to do with Mrs Steiner. The book disappeared after she had been at the desk, clearing away the tea things. Then the intruder let himself in with a key, which I'm willing to bet Mrs Steiner gave him.
ROGER	But Mrs Steiner knows that I would willingly lend her any book in this shop, so why didn't she just ask for the book?
AUBREY	Because she didn't want to be associated with it. Didn't you say that Carlyle's Cromwell was the Prime Minister's favourite book?
ROGER	Yes. But what's that got to do with it?
AUBREY	I think it has great deal to do with it and, if I'm not mistaken, it could be a matter of national – even international – security.

TITANIA	Golly.
AUBREY	Where's that parcel that arrived for Mrs Steiner this morning?*(He starts rummaging through the pile of parcels and letters on the chair. When he finds it, he handles it very gingerly.)* Got it. Didn't her letter say that her husband was going to come and pick up the parcel and her wages?
HELEN	Yes it did.
AUBREY	Right. Well I think we should put this parcel somewhere safe and pretend that it hasn't arrived.
ROGER	Why?
AUBREY	Because I think this parcel is very important to whatever is going on and I think that, if it is not here this morning, they will panic and break in again tonight to get it.
ROGER	Dear me! This all sounds very dangerous. Shouldn't we get the police involved?
AUBREY	I intend to. But first of all, I shall put this parcel away somewhere and I beg all of you to stay well away from it. *(AUBREY holds the parcel out in front of him and carefully takes it into the parlour, opens the window, climbs out and then returns without the parcel.)* There, I've put it under a pile of leaves in your backyard. Stay well away from it.
ROGER	My dear fellow, you're behaving as though it is a bomb or something!
AUBREY	It may very well be. Let's not take any chances shall we? Hold on! *(He spots Mr STEINER coming to the front door.)* Here's the Steiner fellow. Ladies! Go upstairs at once!
	(MR S looks in the shop door. Meanwhile TITANIA and HELEN run "upstairs". ROGER goes swiftly to the desk

and tries to look busy. STEINER comes in the shop.)

STEINER   *(To ROGER)* Mr Mifflin, I have come for my wife's wages and a parcel she was expecting to be delivered.

ROGER   I'm afraid there's been no parcel delivered this morning, Mr Steiner – has there Mr. Gilbert?

AUBREY   No. No parcel.

ROGER   Of course it could come in the second post but we shall be closed by then. I'm afraid you'll have to come back tomorrow, Mr Steiner. I'm sorry for the inconvenience.

STEINER   I can come back at five o'clock tonight, after the second post.

AUBREY   Er…I'm afraid no-one will be here, old chap. We're all going to the cinema, aren't we, Mifflin?

ROGER   Er…yes! The tickets are bought and everything. I shall be open at eight tomorrow morning, though.

STEINER   *(annoyed but having no choice)* Well, tomorrow morning it is, then.

(STEINER glares at AUBREY and leaves.)

AUBREY   I'm pretty sure that was the chap who biffed me over the head last night. He was wearing a balaclava but he was the same build, the same voice, everything.

ROGER   So what happens now?

AUBREY   What happens is that I shall go and see the police about this matter and get them round here. I think you, Mifflin, should shut up shop and take the ladies away for the day.

ROGER   My dear chap! I can't possibly leave you alone to deal with this! I agree about sending the ladies away but… myself? No! For the sake of my books and your friendship, I shall

	stay and keep you company.
AUBREY	It could be very dangerous.
ROGER	I know that. But I cannot, in all conscience, abandon my duties.
AUBREY	Very well. But you must shut up the shop and take the ladies somewhere safe. I think it's best done now. Don't you?
ROGER	Absolutely.
AUBREY	I'll be as quick as I can.

(*AUBREY leaves. ROGER locks the door behind him, puts the key on the desk and then goes to the parlour. He peers out of the window and then draws the curtains. Then he calls "upstairs."*)

ROGER   Helen! Titania! Fetch your hats and coats! I'm taking you somewhere safe!

HELEN   (*offstage*) We'll be right with you!

(*ROGER goes and gets his briefcase and takes it into the parlour. He then takes some papers out of it and starts looking through them. Meanwhile STEINER and WEINTRAUB appear at the front door. WEINTRAUB tries the door and finds it is locked. He steps back and allows STEINER to open the door with a key. STEINER opens the door a crack, puts his hand up to silence the bell and then they creep in. STEINER hangs on to the bell, so that he can close the door quietly and then he locks it. He draws a gun from his pocket and, on hearing voices from the parlour, the two men go behind the front bookcase. HELEN and TITANIA appear from "upstairs". They are wearing hats coats and carrying handbags.*)

HELEN	We're ready dear. Where are you going to take us?
ROGER	I think I shall put you on a train for your sister's house.
HELEN	Oh surely that's a bit extreme, dear! I don't want to be too far away from you.
TITANIA	We could go to my house in Kensington. Of course it means we shall have to explain everything to mother.
ROGER	I think that's a capital idea. Shall we go?
	(They all go into the shop only to find their way barred by the two men, who appear from behind the bookcase. STEINER is pointing a gun.)
MR W	I'm afraid you will have to stay here, Mr Mifflin.
ROGER	Good Lord!
HELEN	Oh My God!
ROGER	How did you get in?
STEINER	With my wife's key, of course. You didn't really think that I accepted your story about the parcel not arriving, did you?
ROGER	Well, no. But we thought you'd come back tonight.
MR W	So that you could lay a trap for us, no doubt. You British really do underestimate everyone else, don't you? You treat the whole world as though they are inferior to you.
TITANIA	*(acidly)* Pardon me, but I thought that was a German trait. At least you seem to have spent the last four years trying to dominate the world.
MR W	And who are you, Fraulein?
TITANIA	Miss Chapman. I work and live here.
MR W	Ah. So you are the fly in the ointment whose unexplained

presence last night disturbed our plans! Where is your
gentleman friend?

TITANIA   I don't know who you mean.

MR W   Come now, Fraulein Chapman, don't waste my time! Where
is the man who shot at Herr Steiner last night and suffered a
severe blow to the head as a result. The man who was here
this morning, so Herr Steiner tells me.

HELEN   He's in the hospital. Mr Steiner here gave him such a bad
head wound, we had to take him to casualty.

STEINER   Rubbish! He was here a moment ago and apart from a
bandage on his head, he seemed fine. And none of you have
had time to take him to a hospital since I left.

ROGER   We put him in a taxi – what does it matter?

MR W   You are quite right Mr Mifflin, it is of no importance. What
is important is what you have done with the package.

ROGER   I told Mr Steiner earlier – it hasn't arrived yet.

MR W   But Herr Steiner and I do not believe you. You see, I was
present when the package was posted and it should have
arrived this morning.

ROGER   (trying to make light of it) Oh well, you know the Post
Office. Since the war, it's been a bit of a shambles.

STEINER   He's lying.

HELEN   This package must be very important if you feel you have to
break in to our shop and hold us at gunpoint.

ROGER   (anxious) Helen…

MR W   Very important. Sit down all of you.

               (MR W motions to the chairs around the desk and ROGER,
               HELEN and TITANIA sit.)

Steiner! Take all their bags away and search them!

(STEINER, still holding the gun on them, takes away ROGER's briefcase and both the women's handbags. He opens each bag and empties the contents on the floor.)

STEINER   Nothing.

MR W   Then I will ask you again, Mr Mifflin. Where is the package?

ROGER   Er…*(having an idea)* Mr Gilbert took it with him!

MR W   Did he? And why would he do that?

ROGER   *(boldly)* He said he was going to take it to the police.

MR W   *(looking at STEINER anxiously)* If he did that, Mr Mifflin, then there will be very grave consequences. You see, if anyone tries to open the book contained in the package, it will explode. I expect we would be able to hear the explosion from here, as the police station is at the end of the street.

ROGER   Good God!

TITANIA   *(being nosy and not able to help herself)* So who was the bomb actually made for then? Who was to be the victim of the explosion?

MR W   *(smiling)* Why your Prime Minister, of course. And, hopefully, the American President who will be in the cabin next door to the Prime Minister on Saturday, when the Isle de France makes the final leg of its journey to France.

ROGER   So that's why you chose Carlyle's Cromwell…

MR W   Of course. The Prime Minister's favourite book, which would have been left on his bedside table by Mrs Steiner, who starts her employment on Saturday as a maid on the ship.

HELEN   I suppose this is all revenge for you being interned as an
               enemy alien?

MR W   *(cross)* You stupid woman! Do you think this is just a petty
               act of personal revenge? This is for the whole of the German
               people! How could we sit by and do nothing while the rest
               of the world meets in Paris to publicly humiliate Germany
               with their Peace Conference? Do you know what they intend
               to do? And what they have done so far?

TITANIA   *(defiantly)* It's no more than the Germans deserve! Dragging
               us all into a dreadful war because of their ambitions!

STEINER   *(advancing on her)* Silence! Or I will shoot you now!

MR W   *(sarcastically)* Oh, you think we should be punished do you?
               Do you think babies should starve as well? And women,
               children and old people?

TITANIA   No, of course not!

MR W   But that's what the Allies have been doing! Ever since
               November, when the war ended, they have systematically
               refused to allow food supplies into Germany. It has been the
               coldest winter in living memory and children have starved
               through it. And, after that, the Allies intend to meet in Paris
               and carve up Germany and its dominions for themselves. Do
               not labour under the naive idea that this war was entered
               into because of only German ambition! Every country that
               came into the war did so because its politicians wanted to
               either make money out of it or grab some land. The treaties
               that the Allies intend to draft in the coming weeks will leave
               Germany penniless, friendless and unable to defend itself.
               This is why the British Prime Minister and the American
               President must die – and anyone else on that ship who is
               part of this so-called Peace Conference.

ROGER	But why did you bring the book back?
STEINER	We only needed the outside covers. If Herr Weintraub had been able to buy the book from you then that would have been all well and good. But my wife stole the book and she knew you would miss it. She was going to return it the next day but she had the accident. So she begged me to return it. No-one would have been any the wiser if you had not interfered.
	(The audience sees AUBREY and the POLICE INSPECTOR appear at the door. MR W and STEINER have their backs to the door. AUBREY makes signs to the INSPECTOR that they should go round the back of the building and they disappear.)
MR W	But I suppose that is typical of the British – always sticking their noses in where they are not wanted. We are running out of time. I shall ask you again. Where is the parcel?
HELEN	And we told you that Mr Gilbert took it with him to the police station.
	(AUBREY and the POLICE INSPECTOR climb in silently through the parlour window. They are both armed.)
MR W	I think not. We have not heard any explosion, have we?
TITANIA	I expect Mr Gilbert told them that it was a bomb and they have not opened it.
MR W	I am tired of these excuses! Steiner! Grab the girl!
	(STEINER grabs TITANIA, who shrieks. He holds her in front of him, his arm round her neck, and points the gun at her head. At the sound of TITANIA's shriek, AUBREY and the POLICE INSPECTOR come through the curtains aiming their guns.)

AUBREY	Let go of her or I'll shoot Weintraub!
INSPECTOR	Let go of the girl!
MR W	Steiner! Keep the girl close! We must not fail now!
STEINER	If you shoot either of us, the girl dies, understand? Put your guns down on the floor. Put them down now, I say!
AUBREY	*(putting his gun on the floor slowly and raising his hands)* As you wish. Don't harm the girl.
STEINER	I said put your gun on the floor, copper!
INSPECTOR	*(copying AUBREY)* Don't be foolish, now. You're already in a lot of trouble, man.
MR W	Mr Gilbert, if you would just tell us where the package is and we will release Miss Chapman. Otherwise, I'm afraid we shall be forced to leave and take her with us. Then we shall kill her and dispose of the body in the river.
TITANIA	Don't tell them Aubrey!
STEINER	Shut your mouth! *(He presses the gun harder into the side of her head)*
AUBREY	*(speaking very quietly and calmly)* There's no need for that. Let the girl go and I'll give you the parcel.
MR W	*(smiling)* Please don't treat us as though we are stupid, Mr Gilbert. The parcel first or the girl dies. It's very simple.
AUBREY	The parcel is in the back yard, under a pile of leaves.
MR W	Steiner. Give me the gun and the girl. You go and look for the parcel.
	(STEINER hands his gun to WEINTRAUB and transfers his arm lock of TITANIA to WEINTRAUB. STEINER then runs through AUBREY and the INSPECTOR and climbs

*through the window. TITANIA, sensing that WEINTRAUB
is not as strong as STEINER sinks her teeth into his arm.
WEINTRAUB yells and releases TITANIA. AUBREY
shouts "Drop!", whilst retrieving his gun. The INSPECTOR
also grabs his gun. TITANIA drops to the floor and the
INSPECTOR fires. WEINTRAUB is hit in the shoulder and
falls. TITANIA grabs his gun.)*

INSPECTOR   Gilbert! Get the other man!

*(AUBREY dashes into the parlour and shouts through the
window, whilst aiming his gun)*

AUBREY   Steiner! Drop the parcel! Steiner!

*(Obviously STEINER tries to run. AUBREY shoots and
there is a massive explosion and flash of light. AUBREY
staggers backwards from the blast and falls to the floor.
HELEN and TITANIA scream. The INSPECTOR runs
into the parlour to check on AUBREY. TITANIA runs after
him.)*

TITANIA   *(fearfully)* Is he dead?

INSPECTOR   No, miss, just unconscious. I'll call for an ambulance. *(The
INSPECTOR goes into the shop and uses the telephone.)*
George! We've got them. Better send an ambulance and
some more PCs. There's a lot of clearing up to be done.
*(WIENTRAUB moans and the INSPECTOR replaces the
phone and goes over to WEINTRAUB)* And you, sir, will be
spending the rest of your life in a British prison.

TITANIA   *(sinking to her knees and cradling AUBREY's head in her
lap.)* Thank God.

*(ROGER and HELEN come into the parlour and look out
of the window)*

HELEN   Oh my God, Roger. There's just a huge hole where our yard
               used to be.

ROGER   Never mind, my dear. At least it wasn't the bookshop.

FADE TO BLACK.

SOUND OF AMBULANCE BELL.

END OF SCENE 3.

THE HAUNTED BOOKSHOP

ACT II

SCENE 4

Three days later. The Bookshop is as it has always been. So is the parlour. ROGER is seated at the desk, writing. TITANIA is dusting the books. HELEN is wrapping a book in brown paper to post.

HELEN   Somehow, I find it difficult to look at a parcel without my hands trembling.

ROGER   *(jumping up)* My dear! Sit yourself down and I will wrap the parcel.

HELEN   Thank you Roger.

(HELEN sits at the desk and ROGER takes over the wrapping of the parcel)

I do wonder how long it takes to get over such a thing? It's been three days now and my ears are still ringing from the bomb blast. And Titania, my dear, you seem absolutely unruffled! When I think of what you went through! Having a gun pressed to your head! It doesn't bear thinking about.

TITANIA   I'm fine! There was a moment, when I thought Aubrey had been killed, that I came over all hysterical…but other than that I thought it was tremendously exciting! Whoever knew that bookselling could be so thrilling!

ROGER   I do hope you don't think bookselling is a life of bombs exploding and men shooting at each other! The most excitement we usually get is when the occasional lady faints from reading Wuthering Heights.

HELEN   Oh we haven't had that happen in a while, dear. Ladies are much tougher nowadays than they used to be.

(AUBREY enters the shop. He still has his head bandaged but he now also has one arm in a sling.)

EVERYONE   Aubrey!

(TITANIA rushes up to him and kisses him on one cheek. He winces a little because she has grabbed his broken arm.)

AUBREY   Ouch! Mind the arm!

TITANIA   Oh, gosh! Sorry, Aubrey! Anyway...what are you doing here? You were supposed to be in hospital until Friday!

AUBREY   Oh I discharged myself. I was going crackers in there. It was so boring and they had no decent books to read.

ROGER   Aha! I sense a sales opportunity there. What do you think, Helen? I could visit the hospital with a suitcase full of books and we could ask the Matron if we could set up a little stall?

HELEN   It sounds a possibility.

ROGER   Of course, I'd have to be very careful in the selection of books. I wouldn't want to set the patient's recovery rate back. They would all have to be either jolly or soothing books – nothing violent or hateful. *(ROGER starts looking around the shelves and making notes.)*

HELEN   Come and sit down, Aubrey and I'll make us all some tea.

(HELEN vacates the chair behind the desk and AUBREY sits down.)

Are you sure you're alright? You look a little pale to me? Doesn't he look pale, Titania?

TITANIA   Yes, he needs looking after.

HELEN	Well, I'll make some tea and you look after him. I think that's the best division of labour.
AUBREY	How's the back yard?
TITANIA	Quite obliterated, I'm afraid.
AUBREY	Oh dear.
ROGER	*(enthusiastically)* No. no, my dear boy. It's all worked out wonderfully well. I was chatting to one of the nice policemen who came and helped tidy things up and his brother is a builder. We're going to extend the shop and build a new parlour where the bomb crater is. So the old parlour will become a reading room and probably house modern novels. *(gravely)* I think the modern books are best kept away from the classics, you know. They don't like them. I think the classical books find the modern novels too brash and pushy. I can positively see them shrinking on the shelves when the modern stuff is put near them.
AUBREY	*(smiling)* It's a relief to see that you're still as dotty as ever, Mifflin. I was afraid that having a bomb go off in your back yard might have changed your personality.
ROGER	*(reassuringly)* Not at all! Not at all! No books were harmed in the episode, that's the main thing. Oh, and of course, the fact that you weren't killed. That was a bonus.
	(MRS CHAPMAN enters the shop. She is smiling and carrying a couple of large envelopes.)
TITANIA	Mummy! What are you doing here? *(she goes up and kisses her mother on the cheek)*
MRS C	Well, I'm the bearer of interesting news. *(she spots AUBREY)* Oh, Mr Gilbert! I'm so glad you're here!

Otherwise I was going to go from here to the hospital.

AUBREY   Is there a problem, Mrs Chapman?

MRS C   Well, I suppose it depends on how you view things...Mr Mifflin! Could I possibly have a look at where the bomb exploded? My husband will be so cross if I don't report back every detail.

ROGER   Of course, of course, I'll take you through!

(ROGER takes MRS C through to the window in the parlour.)

There it is!

MRS C   (peering through the window) My goodness! What a hole! Thank God no-one was hurt!

ROGER   Well, the man who was carrying the bomb was, of course....

MRS C   Was there anything left of him?

ROGER   Very little – but I prefer not to dwell on that, if you don't mind.

MRS C   Quite. (walking back into the shop) It makes me quite faint to think that the bomb could have gone off in the shop!

AUBREY   No, Mrs Chapman. It wouldn't have. It was primed to detonate if the front cover was opened. After all, it had survived the postal system and everything. No, I'm afraid it was me shooting at it that made it explode.

MRS C   Oh I see. You have been extraordinarily heroic, Mr Gilbert.

TITANIA   Yes, he's been wonderful.

MRS C   I wonder if you will find it rather tame to go back to advertising?

AUBREY   Oh no, not at all! I'm looking forward to getting back in the
                saddle, so to speak. A nice quiet, productive existence will
                suit me fine.

MRS C   Mm. That may be a problem...

AUBREY   *(looking worried)* What do you mean?

                (HELEN arrives with a tray of tea things.)

HELEN   Oh Mrs Chapman! Just in time for tea! *(She sets the tray
                down and starts pouring teas, which she hands around.)*

MRS C   I do always seem to turn up at the right time, don't I?

AUBREY   Look here, Mrs Chapman, is there a problem about my job?

MRS C   *(mischievously prolonging the agony)* Well, it appears your
                future at the Grey Matter Advertising Agency is in doubt.

AUBREY   Oh no! Why?

MRS C   Well, my husband, for one, has closed his advertising
                account with them.

AUBREY   *(disappointed)* I suppose it's my fault is it? Putting his
                daughter in danger and all that?

TITANIA   Mummy! Can't you do something? Let me speak to Daddy!

MRS C   *(abandoning all pretence)* Oh it's no good! I can't tease you
                any longer! Mr Gilbert, the reason my husband has
                withdrawn his advertising from the agency is because he
                wants to set up his own advertising department and he
                wants you to head it. *(She gives AUBREY one of the
                envelopes)* Here's a contract, if you would like to take a
                look at it.

AUBREY   *(delighted)* I don't know what to say!

TITANIA   *(hugging her mother)* You darling! Fancy giving poor

Aubrey the collywobbles like that!

MRS C   I know. It was unforgivable but I couldn't resist it. Mr
               Gilbert, my husband and I are so grateful for everything you
               did to protect Titania. Mr Chapman feels it is the least he
               can do to offer you a job with good prospects.

AUBREY   Well, please thank him for me and tell him that I won't let
               him down.

MRS C   I'm sure of that.

ROGER   *(slapping AUBREY on the back)* Well done, dear chap! Well
               done!

MRS C   Now, Mr Mifflin. You needn't think that you've been left
               out of this...

ROGER   Oh?

MRS C   Last week I told my husband about your splendid idea of a
               fleet of mobile bookshops. And Mr Gilbert's also splendid
               idea of buying up unwanted army vehicles. Well, my
               husband being the way he is – never one to pass by a good
               business opportunity – thinks that it is a capital scheme and
               so he's going to start it all up. He wishes to make you a
               partner in the enterprise, along with Titania. If you and she
               organise the stocking of the vans, my husband will organise
               the running of the fleet and the drivers. He's got it all
               worked out and here's a business plan and suggested
               contract for you to look at. *(she hands the other envelope to
               ROGER who looks astounded)*

ROGER   I'm flabbergasted!

HELEN   *(giving ROGER a hug)* It's your lifelong dream, dear! How
               wonderful!

AUBREY	I hope Mr Chapman has suggested that the vans carry an advertisement for ChapmansDaintyBits?
TITANIA	Isn't Aubrey marvellous, Mummy? He's working on behalf of Daddy already!
MRS C	I can assure you that Mr Chapman has thought of the very same thing. I hope you won't mind Mr Mifflin? He thought that each van might have painted upon it "Mifflin's Mobile Bookshop – sponsored by ChapmansDaintyBits"
ROGER	Not at all. I think it's a jolly good thing for commerce to sponsor literature. It's a pity more businessmen don't do it.
HELEN	Well, I think we should all raise our teacups in a toast.
	(They all laugh and do so.)
	What shall the toast be?
AUBREY	That's easy. God Bless the Haunted Bookshop!
EVERYONE	God Bless The Haunted Bookshop!

BLACKOUT

MUSIC

THE END

FURNITURE LIST

Throughout: In the bookstore – bookshelves (front one with removable books – SEE SET PLAN) A small wooden desk with drawers; a wooden chair for the desk; one armchair; at least four wooden chairs dotted about or brought on for various scenes; a candlestick telephone; a cork notice board behind the desk; first aid box containing bandages, a glass bottle of "iodine", cotton wool and safety pins, is in the desk drawer; also a bottle of "aspirin" in the desk drawer.

In the parlour – two armchairs; one coffee table; hat stand in the corner. (Oil lamp optional).

PROPERTY LIST

ACT 1 SCENE 1

Throughout: Books on the desk; a candlestick telephone; a metal cash box; A ledger; a note pad; pencils; sign on the door (SEE SCRIPT). Newspaper on the coffee table in parlour. ROGER's jacket and scarf are on the hatstand.

Page 1:   MRS STEINER enters with a bucket and a cloth.

Page 2:   MRS STEINER takes bucket and cloth offstage. Re-appears with her hat and coat.

Page 3:   AUBREY enters with a briefcase. Business card in his pocket.

Page 7:   MR W enters carrying a paper bag containing a bottle of medicine.

Page 10:   ROGER appears with two plates of toasted cheese.

Page 11:   ROGER appears with two glasses of beer.

Page 14:   ROGER gives AUBREY a copy of Ivanhoe.

ACT 1 SCENE 2

Page 17:	5 chairs need to be assembled in the centre of the stage.
	MRS QUINCY and MRS CHAPMAN have handbags.
	AUBREY has his briefcase.
Page 21:	MRS STEINER enters with a tray containing glasses of cider; A chocolate cake; cloth napkins; forks; small plates and a cake knife.
Page 27:	MRS C produces a book from her handbag.
Page 29:	MRS STEINER enters wearing her hat and coat.
Page 31:	ROGER locks the front door with a key.

ACT 1 SCENE 3

Page 32:	AUBREY enters with a book and his briefcase.
	HELEN enters, wearing a coat and hat and carrying a small suitcase.
Page 33:	HELEN puts her coat and hat on the hat stand and leaves her suitcase in the parlour.
Page 37:	TITANIA enters wearing a hat, carrying a small suitcase and a small bunch of flowers.
Page 38:	TITANIA produces a letter from her suitcase.
Page 40:	AUBREY takes TITANIA'a and HELEN's suitcases offstage.
Page 41:	TITANIA appears holding a notepad and pencil. HELEN exits with the bunch of flowers.
Page 42:	AUBREY exits with his briefcase.
Page 43:	ROGER picks up a large piece of card from the desk.
Page 44:	ROGER pins the card on the notice board.
Page 46:	AUBREY enters the shop *without* his briefcase.

ACT 11 SCENE 1

Page 48:	TITANIA is writing in the ledger. HELEN is packing a small cardboard box with books.
Page 51:	HELEN ties the cardboard box around with string.
Page 54:	MRS C enters with a handbag and wearing hat and gloves.
Page 55:	AUBREY returns with a revolver in his pocket.
Page 56:	HELEN enters with a tray of tea things.
	TITANIA appears with a book.
	AUBREY gives TITANIA money which she puts in the cash box.
Page 59:	AUBREY gives TITANIA the book back and she gives him the money.

ACT 11 SCENE 2

Page 61:	AUBREY is seated in an armchair with the revolver on the table. TITANIA appears with a blanket.
Page 66:	STEINER appears and unlocks the front door with a key. He is carrying a book which he replaces on the shelves.
Page 67:	TITANIA locks the front door with a key from the desk.
	TITANIA gets the first aid box from the desk and takes out some cotton wool, a bottle of iodine, bandage and pins.

ACT 11 SCENE 3.

Page 71:	First aid box, containing a bottle of aspirin and a tray of tea things on the desk.
	Pile of parcels and letters on the armchair by the front door.
Page 72:	ROGER enters, wearing a coat and hat and carrying a briefcase.
Page 74:	ROGER finds the "Cromwell" book on the bookshelves.
Page 76:	AUBREY removes suspect parcel to back yard.
Page 78:	ROGER locks the door after AUBREY leaves. Starts looking through some papers in his briefcase.
	STEINER opens and locks the front door with a key. He draws a gun.
	HELEN and TITANIA appear wearing hats and coats and carrying handbags. (The handbags need to have items in them – SEE SCRIPT) ROGER takes his briefcase through to the shop.
Page 81:	STEINER empties the women's handbags and ROGER's briefcase on the floor.
Page 83:	AUBREY and the POLICE INSPECTOR are carrying guns.

ACT 11 SCENE 4

Page 87:	TITANIA is dusting the books with a duster. HELEN is wrapping a book in brown paper.
Page 88:	AUBREY enters – head bandaged and one arm in a sling.
Page 89:	MRS C enters carrying two large envelopes.
Page 91:	HELEN appears with a tray of tea things.

LIGHTING AND MUSIC

ACT 1	*Opening MUSIC. LIGHTS go up at start of scene.*
SCENE 1	Interior, winter's evening.
	Page 16. CUE: AUBREY: "I shall be here."
	LIGHTS fade to black. MUSIC which continues until…

ACT 1	*LIGHTS go up at start of scene.*
SCENE 2	Interior, winter's evening.
	Page 31: CUE: ROGER: "I'm beginning to think that this book shop really is haunted."
	LIGHTS: Fade to black. MUSIC which continues until…

ACT 1	*LIGHTS go up at start of scene.*
SCENE 3.	Interior, winter's day.
	Page 47: CUE: ROGER: "Thoughts about Carlyle's Cromwell must be pushed aside by beef."
	LIGHTS: Fade to black. Interval MUSIC.

ACT 11	*Opening MUSIC. LIGHTS go up at start of scene.*
SCENE 1	Interior, winter's evening.
	Page 60. CUE: AUBREY: "Good Lord!"
	LIGHTS fade to black. MUSIC which continues until…

ACT 11	*MOONLIGHT through window and door, allowing*
SCENE 2	*some light on actors in the parlour.*
	Interior, night.

Page 67: TITANIA turns on the shop lights.

LIGHTS: *instant interior illumination.*

Page 70: CUE: AUBREY: "I'm not that wounded…"

LIGHTS *fade to black.* MUSIC *which continues until…*

ACT 11
SCENE 3

LIGHTS *go up at start of scene.*

Interior, day.

Page 85: CUE: AUBREY: Gunshot.

LIGHTS: *flash of explosion offstage left, seen through window.*

Page 86: CUE: ROGER: "At least it wasn't the bookshop."

LIGHTS *fade to black.* No MUSIC *just ambulance bells (See EFFECTS)*

ACT 11
SCENE 4

LIGHTS *go up at start of scene.*

Interior, day.

Page 93: CUE: EVERYONE: "God Bless the Haunted Bookshop!"

LIGHTS *fade to black. Closing* MUSIC *and* CURTAIN CALLS.

EFFECTS

(It is advisable that the set is fitted with an overhead bell on the front door. If this is too difficult, then the idea of a shop door bell could be abandoned completely.)

ACT 1
SCENE 1

Page 9:   CUE: ROGER: "I shan't be long"

           SFX: Telephone rings until AUBREY answers it.

ACT 1
SCENE 3

Page 45:   CUE: ROGER: "…have another look for that Cromwell book."

           SFX: telephone rings until ROGER answers it.

ACT 11
SCENE 1

Page 51:   CUE: HELEN: "I think Roger's insanity may be catching."

           SFX : telephone rings until TITANIA answers it.

ACT 11
SCENE 2

Page 66:   CUE: AUBREY: "Stop where you are! I have a gun!"

           SFX: one gunshot.

ACT 11

SCENE 3

Page 85:   CUE: AUBREY: "Steiner! Drop the parcel! Steiner!"

SFX: One gunshot, followed by loud explosion offstage.

Page 86:   CUE: ROGER: "Never mind, my dear. At least it wasn't the book shop."

SFX: Ambulance bell or bells.

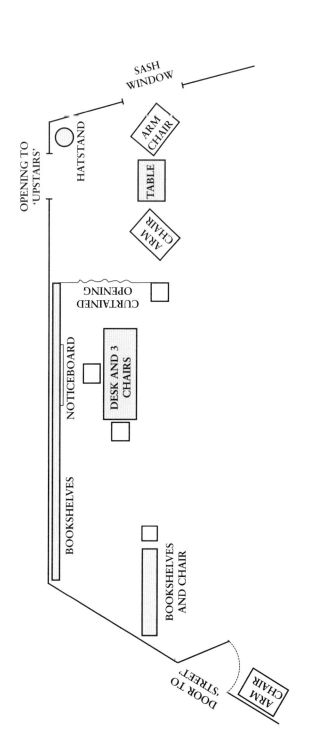

THE HAUNTED BOOKSHOP – SET PLAN, AERIAL VIEW

SASH
WINDOW

OPENING TO
'UPSTAIRS'

HATSTAND

ARM
CHAIR

TABLE

ARM
CHAIR

CURTAINED
OPENING

NOTICEBOARD

DESK AND 3
CHAIRS

BOOKSHELVES

BOOKSHELVES
AND CHAIR

DOOR TO
'STREET'

ARM
CHAIR